CITY BY DESIGN

an architectural perspective of dallas

Published by

PANACHE
PANACHE PARTNERS, LLC

1424 Gables Court
Plano, Texas 75075
469.246.6060
Fax: 469.246.6062
www.panache.com

Publishers: Brian G. Carabet and John A. Shand
Executive Publisher: Steve Darocy
Senior Associate Publishers: Martha Cox and Karla Setser
Editors: Rosalie Wilson and Ryan Parr
Senior Designer: Ben Quintanilla

Printed in Malaysia

Distributed by Independent Publishers Group
800.888.4741

PUBLISHER'S DATA

City by Design Dallas
Library of Congress Control Number: 2007930828

ISBN 13:   978-1-933415-41-3
ISBN 10:   1-933415-41-X

First Printing 2008

10 9 8 7 6 5 4 3 2 1

Previous Page: Victory Tower, BOKA Powell, page 272
Rendering by Crystal CG

This Page: RadioShack Riverfront Campus, HKS, Inc., page 208
Photograph by Blake Marvin/HKS, Inc.

CITY BY DESIGN

an architectural perspective of dallas

FOREWORD

by Paula Clements, Executive Director, AIA Dallas

Once envisioned as a mere trading post, the Dallas area, upon being discovered by settlers, did not remain a secret for long. By the late-1800s it gained renown as a popular place to put down roots and was at one point the largest city in the state. Today, Dallas is a destination rich in history, culture and architecture. The natural and built environments commingle for a breathtaking display that continues to draw people from across the United States and various corners of the globe.

Dallas teems with sublime architectural achievements, and opportunities abound for experiencing exceptional building design. With four Pritzker award-winning architects designing buildings in the Dallas Arts District and numerous other talented professionals gracing the cityscape with their creativity, Dallas attracts residents as well as visitors, who come just to catch a glimpse of and study the city's structures.

FACING PAGE: Dallas' majestic skyline begs to be explored.
Photograph by Justin Terveen

To celebrate and further solidify Dallas' identity as an architectural hot spot, the leadership of the Dallas chapter of the American Institute of Architects conceived of the idea for the Dallas Center for Architecture, then conferred with likeminded leaders of the Dallas Architectural Foundation and the Dallas Architecture Forum to create the venue, which will undoubtedly highlight the unique array of world-class architecture that comprises this vibrant urban landscape. For the time being, the center is housed with AIA Dallas' headquarters and has an accompanying virtual resource, dallascfa.org, replete with an events calendar, case studies of award-winning buildings and information on new architectural accomplishments, among other things. In coming years it will be realized three-dimensionally with exhibit areas, a library and gathering spaces for enjoyment by architects, design aficionados and those who have yet to discover the full beauty of this venerable and prodigious artistic pursuit.

LEFT: The surrounding works of architecture echo the vibrancy that the DART light rail train brings to downtown Dallas.
Photograph by Justin Terveen

FACING PAGE LEFT: Striking material combinations enrich the city's architectural fabric.
Photograph by Justin Terveen

FACING PAGE RIGHT: Each pane of glass glows resplendently at sunset.
Photograph by Justin Terveen

The goal of the center is twofold: to offer architects, urban planners and their affiliates a forum where they can interact and share ideas, and to procure even greater public interest in the architecture that defines Dallas and welcomes its visitors. The developing and strengthening of collaborative ties is another intended benefit of the center. Relationships among allied organizations and academic communities will be strengthened, and industry professionals' influence on public policy regarding issues of sustainable community planning and the built environment will be elevated. In short, it will promote the intrinsic value of quality architecture in Dallas and in its surrounding communities.

The vast majority of the projects featured within this *City by Design Dallas* collection were crafted by members—many of whom are native Dallasites—of the three organizations that have come together to create the Dallas Center for Architecture. Their commitment to enhancing the city with aesthetically pleasing, innovative and timeless buildings is clear in the passionate manner in which they share their lives' work, and is further evidenced by the works of architecture themselves—the built environment in which people enjoy living, working and relaxing.

LEFT: The brilliant work of Dallas architects is nicely complemented by the creativity of others.
Photograph by Justin Terveen

RIGHT: Dallas' iconic Reunion Tower, designed by a California-based firm in the 1970s, can be enjoyed from many vantage points.
Photograph by Justin Terveen

Victory Tower, BOKA Powell, page 272

INTRODUCTION

Each day, we pass by hundreds of buildings—a mélange of old and new works of architecture—that we likely take for granted, not for lack of interest but because life's frenetic pace often prohibits asking why, how, when and through whose creativity did the built environment around us come to fruition. Yet it is these very structures, unassuming or prominently placed, that create the brilliantly complex urban and suburban landscapes where our lives unfold.

Imagine being afforded the rare opportunity to gaze inside the walls and around the perimeter of these buildings that are equal parts mysterious, familiar and alluring. Imagine meeting their creators and discovering the forward-thinking design savvy behind the selection of each material, the placement of each door and window, the sculptural use of both classical and contemporary architectural forms. Now turn the page—commence an invigorating journey that is sure to ignite your appreciation or renew your passion for Dallas' architectural fabric.

You will immediately discern *City by Design Dallas* as unique among architectural collections. Indeed, it boasts vibrant photographs of stimulating designs melded with insightful editorial, yet it does not endeavor to present merely the tallest, widest, newest, oldest or Greenest buildings. More precisely, it is a rich, diverse collection of the city's best—from landmark skyscrapers that define Dallas' majestic skyline to smaller, thoughtfully designed edifices of some of the suburbs' best-kept secrets. It is a regional compilation of masterfully conceived structures considered preeminent by the locally based architects and developers who have turned intangible ideas into built realities that will be enjoyed for generations to come.

RadioShack Riverfront Campus, HKS, Inc., page 208

CONTENTS

Omni Fort Worth Hotel & Condominiums,
Hellmuth, Obata + Kassabaum (HOK), page 256

CHAPTER ONE
Built to Play and Stay

From early morning to afternoon, evening and night, the city swirls about with activity. At the heart of this vibrant energy are its retail, hospitality, dining and recreation establishments, be they classically inspired structures, crisp displays of modern architecture or a happy medium between the two.

Out-of-town guests have their pick of some of the nation's most exclusive resort-like settings such as Three's Hotel Palomar and HKS' W Dallas Victory Hotel, and locals, too, reserve the right to enjoy a lavish overnight stay every once in a while. Whether lounging in the Caribbean-style ambience of Life's a Beach Grill designed by NCA Partners or in the ultra-posh GhostBar, the W Hotel's chic rooftop venue, numerous restaurant and recreation options exist throughout the streets of downtown and neighboring suburbs.

The savviest of boutique-company entrepreneurs recognize and appreciate the value in working with architects to define their style and present a prominent image to the world, while the masterminds behind nationally run entities have already witnessed, firsthand, the power of carefully crafted architecture. The designs of these engaging and, at times, whimsical venues showcase the innovative nature of their architects.

Belmont Hotel, Options Real Estate Development,
johnson/twitmyer joint venture, Hocker Design Group, page 22

Nobu Restaurant, CamargoCopeland Architects, LLP, page 16

W Dallas Victory Hotel & Residences, HKS, Inc., page 42

Nobu Restaurant

■ ■

CamargoCopeland Architects, LLP

■ ■ ■ ■ ■ ■ ■ ■ ■ ■ ■ Collaborating with Shawn Sullivan of Rockwell Group, CamargoCopeland Architects' E.J. Copeland, AIA, NCARB, and Roberto Diaz, Associate AIA, utilized their vast architectural experience to overcome unique challenges and effectively install the critically acclaimed Japanese-themed restaurant, Nobu, into Dallas' Hotel Crescent Court. Encapsulating the unique ambience of restaurateur Nobu Matsuhisa's wildly successful and swiftly expanding entrée into contemporary Japanese cuisine—while simultaneously utilizing dynamic and wholly unique design elements— Rockwell Group as the design architect captured the essence of a Nobu restaurant and together with CamargoCopeland as the architect of record recreated it with a singular vision right in North Texas.

FACING PAGE: Scorched ash, cut steel and silk fabrics define the main dining room of the restaurant and provide a dynamic backdrop to Nobu Matsuhisa's culinary creations.
Photograph by David Joseph Photography

Working within a preexisting space in the Hotel Crescent that had formerly been home to the Beau Nash restaurant, the designers were faced with the prospect of implementing an elaborate plan in a space that had not been renovated in more than 20 years. Further complicating matters, Beau Nash's kitchen area previously operated as the hotel's room-service kitchen, which had to be separated from the Nobu construction in order to continue to serve that function. Moreover, the construction needed to commence subtly, so as not to disturb hotel patrons—many of whom are professional athletes with uncommon sleep schedules—all while on a very tight deadline.

The Rockwell Group and CamargoCopeland team implemented a pure design concept capturing the intended Japanese aesthetic, interpreting it in a very elegant and engaging fashion. For example, the lighting inside Nobu was designed and detailed in a clean, precise manner so that the light grazes fabric panels as they hang down to create more drama. As is the case with the pendant/hanging fixtures, the lights, which are enclosed with actual fishing baskets, lend an air of authenticity to the space and reinforce Nobu's Japanese cultural aesthetic.

Supplementing that exceptionally focused lighting scheme, the project's design team utilized an assortment of honest, organic materials in a sophisticated manner to create a stately ambience. Wood, stone and metal comprise most

LEFT: Lounge seating is anchored by wooden shelves influenced by the Japanese Tokonoma and a modern interpretation of the shoji screen.
Photograph by David Joseph Photography

FACING PAGE LEFT: Cherry blossoms, silk curtains and black slate adorn the garden room and provide a serene and tranquil escape from the dynamic dining room.
Photograph by David Joseph Photography

FACING PAGE RIGHT: Underlit birch twigs separate the dining area from Nobu's display kitchen, which is anchored by a wall of black river stones.
Photograph by David Joseph Photography

of the material elements and are used in various innovative ways that include blackened steel plates used as column wraps, onyx lighting panels, end-grain sliced and oiled wood floors and flamed-ash wood veneer throughout.

Culturally significant elements were interjected throughout the space to further accentuate Nobu's one-of-a-kind character. Lotus leaves adorn the inside of glass windows in addition to the use of bamboo in the main entrance area. Black river rocks anchor the main back wall and further enhance Nobu's earthy aura.

This Rockwell/CamargoCopeland collaboration effectively and innovatively infused Nobu's unique ambience with appropriate yet compelling design details that have made the Dallas location a destination unto itself. Consequently, the city has embraced the presence of an internationally recognized, premier restaurant that places Dallas on the short list of fine-dining locales. ■ ■ ■ ■ ■ ■ ■ ■ ■ ■ ■

RIGHT: Inspired by Japanese chochin, the sushi bar lighting invites customers to sit at the backlit onyx bar.
Photograph by David Joseph Photography

FACING PAGE: The backlit bar, texturally reminiscent of tatami mats, highlights Nobu's premium sake selections.
Photograph by David Joseph Photography

Belmont Hotel

■ ■

Options Real Estate Development
johnson/twitmyer joint venture
Hocker Design Group

■ ■ ■ ■ ■ ■ ■ ■ ■ ■ ■ The Belmont Hotel has done more than its fair share of bringing hip to Dallas. With unparalleled style and flair, this renovated 1940s' motor inn sits proudly on a stone embankment in north Oak Cliff, offering one of the most spectacular views of the Dallas skyline. The main Art Moderne building, with its smartly renovated interiors, is accompanied by thoughtful landscaping, garden rooms, loft suites, bungalows, a stunningly tiled pool and an ultra-swanky lounge—popular with artsy locals and guests. Charming walkways and gardens provide views and inspiration around the four-acre terraced site.

Options Real Estate developer Monte Anderson frequently visited the Belmont Motor Hotel restaurant during his childhood. The motel, originally a vision of renowned architect Charles Stevens Dilbeck, held a mysterious charm that remained with Monte into adulthood. This memory, and a spectacular view

FACING PAGE: Native vegetation enhances the hotel's idyllic setting.
Project Design Team: Monte Anderson, Sally Johnson, Carole Twitmyer, David Hocker, Jack Hammack and Lena Liles.
Photograph by Scott Jenke

of downtown Dallas, prompted him to purchase the adjacent vacant land. Monte's subsequent visit to Austin's San Jose Hotel inspired his vision for the Belmont and an adjacent new urbanist community. The developer commissioned a close-knit team, including lead architect Sally Johnson and landscape architect David Hocker, who infused their quirky, fun-loving spirit into the Belmont Hotel. General manager Lena Liles maintains this high-spirited atmosphere on a daily basis and adds yet another dynamic personality into the mix.

The renovation maintains the motor court's original integrity and appeal from 1946. The design team restored the original window openings, using aluminum windows styled per the original drawings. Today the hotel combines 1950s' style with a contemporary flair. Bright blue tiles and eclectic furnishings subtly transport guests into a relaxed state while still enjoying an array of modern luxuries. Flat–screen televisions, wireless internet access, the Belmont Health Club, Cliff Café and Lather toiletries are all available to oblige hotel clientele.

Perhaps the hotel's success is so fulfilling to the team because of the tremendous amount of adversity that arose with the proposition of renovation. With difficult soil requirements, poor zoning, outdated electrical wiring and Oak Cliff's less-than-perfect reputation, the involved parties met continual resistance. The passion and tenacity of the group, however, pulled the project through, resulting in a restoration that has brought a sense of pride to the entire community. This once run-down motor hotel is the cornerstone of a 14-acre mixed-use development connecting the area to downtown. ■ ■ ■ ■ ■ ■ ■ ■ ■ ■ ■ ■

TOP LEFT: Clean lines and vibrant colors set the stage for a pleasant experience.
Photograph by Scott Jenke

BOTTOM LEFT: Designed by David Hocker, RLA, ASLA, the glass-mosaic fountain wall and native, adaptive plantings give a contemporary feel to a historic setting.
Photograph by Gisela Borghi

FACING PAGE LEFT: Reminiscent of a Texas ranch, a water-trough fountain bubbles in one of several meditative courtyards on the four-acre grounds.
Photograph by Gisela Borghi

FACING PAGE RIGHT: A steep hillside becomes more dramatic with a mass planting of fountain grass, swaying from even the slightest wind. The hilltop location enjoys both views and breezes.
Photograph by Gisela Borghi

Fort Worth Convention Center

Hellmuth, Obata + Kassabaum (HOK)

■ ■ ■ ■ ■ ■ ■ ■ ■ ■ Aiming to reintegrate the 1960s-built Fort Worth Convention Center into the context of the city's vibrant downtown district while fulfilling its expanded programmatic needs, HOK, as the design architect, astutely implemented a 300,000-square-foot renovation and expansion, effectively invigorating the convention center's economic potential as well as enhancing the urban fabric of the city.

A key tenet of the renovation consisted of seamlessly integrating the new convention facility with the adjacent Fort Worth Water Gardens, designed by architect Phillip Johnson, which is an enchanting urban park with relaxing water features. An important element of this strategy was the closing

FACING PAGE: Integrating the convention center with the nearby Water Gardens was a key component of HOK's expansion/renovation.
Project Design Team: Kirk Millican, Sandra Paret, Steven Janeway and Tim Gaiddis.
Photograph by Craig D. Blackmon, FAIA

of an existing city street to create a generous plaza area allowing for event scheduling between the two spaces. Situating the convention center's new 30,000-square-foot grand ballroom to the south, HOK took advantage of this opportunity to create a dramatic entrance forecourt. Once inside, an elegant two-story atrium, with a view overlooking the Water Gardens, graciously connects to the second-floor ballroom utilizing two monumental staircases.

Another site consideration influencing the design was the creation of a pedestrian thoroughfare utilizing a long linear façade along Houston Street that could be outfitted with retail storefronts connecting Main Street to the north. By bringing the convention center's western exterior directly to the curb and concluding side streets at major entries, the nearly 1,000-foot linear façade is conceptually broken into blocks. A prominent tower at the building's southwest corner, framed with the motif of a Texas star, illuminates brightly at night and acts as a focal point for the intersection of the south and west façades.

Respectful of the city's existing architecture, the convention center incorporates double-hung windows and window bays, while employing distinctive brick patterns and colors, façade proportions, styles and detailing to create a unique and enduring architecture inspired by the Fort Worth vernacular. The one-of-a-kind styling is carried inside as interior spaces relate to the city's storied past, drawing from Fort Worth's rich cultural, historical and geographical contexts. The grand ballroom, for example, summons a West Texas sky and landscape with a carpet of Texas wildflowers under a ceiling composed of 53 resplendent, hanging silver stars.

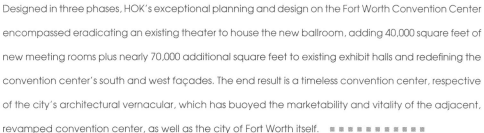

Designed in three phases, HOK's exceptional planning and design on the Fort Worth Convention Center encompassed eradicating an existing theater to house the new ballroom, adding 40,000 square feet of new meeting rooms plus nearly 70,000 additional square feet to existing exhibit halls and redefining the convention center's south and west façades. The end result is a timeless convention center, respective of the city's architectural vernacular, which has buoyed the marketability and vitality of the adjacent, revamped convention center, as well as the city of Fort Worth itself. ■ ■ ■ ■ ■ ■ ■ ■ ■ ■ ■

ABOVE LEFT: An elegant two-story atrium, which overlooks the nearby Water Gardens, and monumental stair funnel patrons to the second-floor grand ballroom.
Photograph by Craig D. Blackmon, FAIA

ABOVE RIGHT: An interior ceiling view of the prominent tower, framed with the motif of a Texas star, defines the convention center's southwest corner.
Photograph by Craig D. Blackmon, FAIA

FACING PAGE TOP: Respective of Fort Worth's existing architectural vernacular, the convention center features double-hung windows and window bays as well as distinctive brick patterns and colors, façade proportions, styles and detailing.
Photograph by Craig D. Blackmon, FAIA

FACING PAGE BOTTOM: The building's long, linear western façade along Houston Street was broken into blocks by concluding side streets at major entries, providing valuable space for retail storefronts.
Photograph by Craig D. Blackmon, FAIA

Hotel Palomar

■ ■

Three

■ ■ ■ ■ ■ ■ ■ ■ ■ ■ ■   Before Hotel Palomar, lobbies were simply check-in points, pool areas were only enjoyed from several stories up and rooms were used exclusively with the lights off.

Under the creative direction of Gary Koerner, founder and principal of internationally celebrated Three, the 198-room hotel and adjacent residential tower—as well as the hip restaurant, bar, boutique shops and spa—sprung from the modest origins of a 1960s' property and was reintroduced nearly half a century later as a new Dallas landmark, a place to see and be seen.

FACING PAGE: A feeling of openness is encouraged by Texas sunlight gleaming through 26-foot windows encasing the first floor. Cylindrical amber glass pendants suspend gracefully above a cantilevered stair.
Project Design Team: Gary P. Koerner and Rob Lara. Interior design by Cheryl Rowley and Bob LaCour; restaurant design by Paul Draper.
Photograph by David Phelps

"The hotel itself is the 'living room' of the entire development," describes Gary, and many feel that the development as a whole acts as a "living room" for the surrounding Highland Park and SMU communities, as its presence has had a profound, revitalizing influence. Sophisticated and welcoming, an attenuated water feature graces the front façade and is mirrored inside, creating an immediate indoor-outdoor connection and a sense of tranquility that is further enhanced by the thoughtful material palette, earth-toned color scheme, repeated geometric forms and, of course, strong, clean architectural lines.

While Palomar definitely has a serene quality, it also possesses a certain vibrancy that attracts and welcomes a generational blend of residents, guests and neighbors. Its creators are deeply satisfied that 20-year-olds and 70-year-olds, alike, enjoy the ambience, atmosphere and sense of community that is Palomar. People need not know why the space feels right, only that it does. The attractive residential scale was achieved through superb master planning, pedestrian-proportioned spaces, a hidden below-grade garage and smart interior layouts.

The four-star result of close collaboration among a group of talented professionals, Palomar came to fruition as Dallas' first urban resort, mixed-use development and has raised the standard of luxury. Palomar has a commanding presence yet subtly pays homage to the original architecture of Ralph Kelman, which remains at the heart of the new community. Designs of

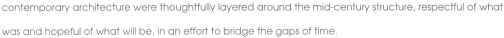

contemporary architecture were thoughtfully layered around the mid-century structure, respectful of what was and hopeful of what will be, in an effort to bridge the gaps of time.

Like many Dallasites, the structure from whence Palomar came had sentimental value to Three's founder, who celebrated his marriage at the original location and fondly recalls dining at adjacent Trader Vic's as a child. In architecturally preserving those memories, the architects set the stage for new memories to be made in coming years. Every project undertaken by Three is significant and unique in its own right—and its repertoire of projects spans six continents—yet Palomar is the embodiment of the breathtaking boutique architecture for which the firm is so well known. ■ ■ ■ ■ ■ ■ ■ ■ ■

ABOVE LEFT: Dramatic drapery panels frame a covered loggia lounge in a widely scaled black and white horizontal stripe. Teak sofas make an impression with an exaggerated high back comprised of vertical steel rods and tightly woven chocolate resin.
Photograph by David Phelps

ABOVE RIGHT: The rich neutral guest room palette is energized by graphic elements and vibrant yellow accents. Geometric shapes interact in subtle and dominant motifs, reminiscent of architectural elements throughout the hotel.
Photograph by David Phelps

FACING PAGE TOP: Ralph Kelman's architectural design of the existing 1960s' hotel provided modern inspiration for the hotel renovation and complementary residential tower designed by Three.
Photograph by Craig D. Blackmon, FAIA

FACING PAGE BOTTOM LEFT: The residential tower defines urban living with a private entrance and large balconies boasting views of downtown Dallas, Southern Methodist University and the Katy Trail.
Photograph by Craig D. Blackmon, FAIA

FACING PAGE BOTTOM RIGHT: The courtyard in the center of the resort provides guests and residents access to four-star dining, Texas' first mind and body spa, the infinity-edge pool or the open-air pavilion fireplace.
Photograph by Craig D. Blackmon, FAIA

Life's a Beach Grill & Sports Bar

NCA Partners

■ ■ ■ ■ ■ ■ ■ ■ ■ ■ Eating out at an exceptional restaurant encompasses more than just great food—when consummated effectively, dining out engenders an opportunity to disconnect from life's daily routine and relax for a few hours with friends and family. Designed by NCA Partners led by Lance Rose, Life's a Beach Grill & Sports Bar procures an authentic Caribbean feel, affording patrons a place to enjoy their own miniature island vacation right in North Texas.

In 2005, the owners of Life's a Beach began collaborating with NCA to bring a slice of their beloved Caribbean to the Metroplex and create a one-of-a-kind environment. Located in the quiet neighborhood of Highland Village, Life's a Beach reaps the benefits of an isolated setting with pleasant water features in back of the restaurant, which separate the site from adjacent recreation fields. Rarely does a restaurant's exterior setting receive as much

FACING PAGE: Vibrant colors, an outdoor bar and ample deck seating provide a buoyant exterior setting for enjoying Life's a Beach's effervescent ambience.
Photograph by John Benoist

attention as its interior, but creating a functional outdoor environment with a convincing tropical aura was a top priority. Outdoor patio areas provide seating for 200 patrons and feature open deck areas with intermittent sand, thatched umbrellas, arbors and trelliswork, wooden piers with gooseneck lanterns and a sand beach with a pair of spacious volleyball courts. A circular, open fire pit serves as a focal point of the serpentine deck area and rock formations replete with waterfalls provide an enchanting backdrop, resulting in a resort-style ambience.

That engrossing outdoor character is further embellished by the rich colors integrated into the building's stucco exterior. So captivating were the prolific blues, reds and yellows, in addition to the ample outdoor area, curious patrons frequented and inquired about the unopened restaurant to the point that the owners finally opened early and were met with lines out the door. The tropical aura that permeates the outdoor patios was brought inside the restaurant through a tall entryway that has a raised-hut feel, in addition to abundant windows, French doors and indoor fireplaces. Moreover, the main dining room utilizes a trussed, open ceiling with clerestory at the top, large fans and

chandeliers covered in grass cloth. Table tops are comprised of coconut husks, which are accented by colorful, floral fabrics in the furniture. Bamboo-inlaid panels outfit the front of the bar, which offers a slightly more effervescent atmosphere than the rest of the restaurant.

Crafting a vibrant edifice that encapsulates the tropical grandeur desired by Life's a Beach's owners, NCA Partners created a family-friendly destination that allows patrons to get away from the daily grind in a delightful outdoor setting that brings a little piece of the Caribbean to the North Texas area. ■ ■ ■ ■ ■ ■ ■ ■ ■ ■ ■

Village Country Club

■ ■

Harry C. Hoover Jr. Architects and Planners

■ ■ ■ ■ ■ ■ ■ ■ ■ ■ When Harry Hoover began designing the Village Country Club in the late '60s, no one could have possibly known the

tremendous success that would ensue. Today, the 18,000-square-foot country club serves more than 10,000 residents who enjoy living near downtown

Dallas in the prestigious development of 14 distinct apartment communities.

Tasked to design a multipurpose facility with a robust Germanic/Bavarian personality on a conservative budget, Harry began as he always does: with

a relaxed mindset, allowing the needs of the building to fall together, looking for solutions within problems and reworking designs until the building

ABOVE: The sizeable, two-foot by three-foot color rendering was created with a combination of watercolor and tempera.
Rendering courtesy of Harry C. Hoover Jr. Architects and Planners

FACING PAGE: Enveloped in mature-growth trees, the club's gracious circular driveway provides a point of welcome, drawing in residents and their guests just as beautifully as when the trees were a bit smaller, nearly four decades ago.
Photograph by Ben Quintanilla

starts to express itself. In response to the development's Village appellation, which implies a group of buildings clustered together, Harry's solution utilized a logical flow of spaces to give an attitude suggesting a group of buildings in a small "village," which gave identity to the separate but related functions. That produced the various proportionate ceiling heights resulting in the "village look" of the undulating rooflines.

The boisterous German beer hall attitude manifested itself throughout the building with the architect's selection of stained oak beams, strong brick masses, substantial trim work, thoughtful detailing and a profusion of warm, invigorating colors and textures. A gracious vestibule provides access to each of the club's main areas, connecting the beer garden/bar/billiard lounge, Olympic-size pool and cabana to the great hall, and the bar/dining space to the spa, exercise room, lockers, golf/tennis pro shops and management offices.

Harry came about this unique design opportunity through his construction consultation work. So practiced is he in his profession that third-party organizations, such as banks, call on him to monitor the construction progress of their investments, and law firms seek his consultation in design and construction matters for litigation purposes. This seasoned professional has earned the confidence of industry peers and clients alike; in fact, one client insists that

TOP LEFT: The expansive Village Country Club boasts varied rooflines that house myriad amenities.
Photograph by Ben Quintanilla

BOTTOM LEFT: Brilliantly illuminated at night, luxurious cabana and lounge areas are adjacent to the Olympic-size pool.
Photograph by Ben Quintanilla

FACING PAGE: A four-way fireplace, adorned with brick from floor to pitched ceiling, graces the beer garden/bar/lounge/game area. Recalling the flavor of Bavarian-style architecture, natural light enters the space through the dormer.
Photograph courtesy of Harry C. Hoover Jr. Architects and Planners

her woodworker husband should not touch anything in their Harry Hoover-designed home without the architect's blessing.

Works of architecture created by Harry C. Hoover Jr. Architects and Planners, such as the Village Country Club, appeal to a broad audience because rather than limiting himself to one or two fleeting styles, the principal focuses on creating attitudes consistent with the building's function, thereby developing a one-of-a-kind solution that is neither stereotyped nor locked in time, but rather continues to grow in value to the owner in many ways—not only accommodating the functional and physical needs but the needs of the spirit. These same principles apply to community-oriented projects and institutional, commercial and residential commissions as well.

He is also interested in historical preservation work and has resided in University Park's oldest house, a 1915-built Prairie style, for the nearly half a century. Over the years, Harry has made reasonable adjustments and enhancements to allow the building to evolve into present times but safeguarded the home's attitude and soul. *Better Homes and Gardens* once described his work as exemplary of a fresh style not yet named and applauded the open floor plan and freedom of expression it afforded. It is this absence of superficial style, but presence of personality that fosters successful attitudes and functions in each architectural design. ■ ■ ■ ■ ■ ■ ■ ■ ■ ■ ■

W Dallas Victory Hotel & Residences

HKS, Inc.

■ ■ ■ ■ ■ ■ ■ ■ ■ ■ ■ Victory Park, the 75-acre, master-planned urban district within downtown Dallas, is already teeming with development and rife with activity—just a few short years since construction on this innovative neighborhood commenced. While the American Airlines Center was unequivocally the first major component of this burgeoning development, the nearby W Dallas Victory Hotel & Residences represents Victory's first prominent mixed-use construction as well as a catalyst for a more modern architectural vernacular in this progressive precinct.

The American Airlines Center officially opened in July 2001, marking an exciting new era for the city of Dallas characterized by the ensuing Victory Park development. Despite serving as the first symbol of Victory development, the AAC featured a more conservative, traditional style marked by sweeping brick

FACING PAGE: The stylish, 33-story W Hotel is the Dallas skyline's recent iconic addition.
Project Design Team: Nunzio DeSantis, Eddie Abeyta, Brad Schrader and Karen Yeoman.
Photograph by HKS/Blake Marvin

façades and smooth arches. In 2003, when the W was in its nascent planning stages, HKS envisioned a modern style, fitting of the W Hotel brand, which would also champion a more progressive approach in future Victory development.

HKS knew that the W was intended to have a strong relationship with and serve as a focal point to the heavily trafficked plaza area outside the AAC. Thus, employing the grand vision that characterizes all of HKS' work, the project team drew an analogy of the W serving as a landmark to the plaza outside the AAC—as well as the larger Victory Park development—in the same way that the Campanile di San Marco in Venice, Italy, acts as an iconic centerpiece to the Piazza San Marco.

Brilliantly designed and constructed on a fast-track schedule, the 33-story W is already an iconic landmark in the Dallas skyline—the type of remarkable edifice that is instantly associated with the city. Replete with more than 250 high-end W Hotel rooms, 150 luxury condominiums, five-star spa and fitness facilities, upscale bar and restaurant scenes and ample retail opportunities, the W has been gloriously received and certainly exceeded all expectations.

LEFT: A notch in the building's massing on the 16th floor provides an outdoor, infinity-edge pool that is enjoyed by hotel guests and condo residents alike.
Photograph by HKS/Blake Marvin

FACING PAGE TOP: The W shines in the night sky and provides a stark contrast to the adjacent American Airlines Center.
Photograph by HKS/Blake Marvin

FACING PAGE BOTTOM: Immaculate downtown views make the communal outdoor pool area a highly desired leisure spot.
Photograph by HKS/Blake Marvin

One of the more unique design elements incorporated into the W is the outdoor infinity-edge pool located on the 16th floor. A notch in the building's massing, the pool deck serves as a common zone between the hotel and condo divisions as it separates the two and is shared by both. It also provides patrons with an elevated, outdoor observation deck with full afternoon sun exposure, providing unmatched downtown views. Those immaculate views are further engendered throughout the luxury condominium units, which feature 10-foot, floor-to-ceiling glass, in addition to eight-foot-deep cantilevered balconies that extend the length of the condo and function as outdoor living rooms.

Impeccably conceptualized and crafted by HKS, the W Dallas Victory Hotel & Residences will be remembered as the first major mixed-use component of Victory Park, an iconic structure in the Dallas skyline and as the impetus for ensuing Victory development. ■ ■ ■ ■ ■ ■ ■ ■ ■ ■

CHAPTER TWO
Urban Living

Urban living has been revitalized in many cities that had once lost much of their vitality to urban sprawl, resulting in a recharged ambience, buildings bustling about with activity and convenient access to downtown living and working. These pages represent the finest examples of how an architectural vision can transform and improve the landscape and quality of life for city dwellers.

Whether it is a mixed-use building that combines residential units and retail space or a multifamily residence cropping up in place of abandoned buildings or land, the firms involved in these substantial projects undertake not only the logistics of planning, creating and executing the design, they realize the impact their project will have on the growth and success of their native city. Dallas residences like Architecture Demarest's Magnolia Hill, Beeler Guest Owens Architects' 5225 Maple and Gromatzky Dupree & Associates' The Ashton are sure to impress.

The architects' diverse attitudes and thoughts behind their buildings may fascinate or even surprise. One aspect that weaves a common thread throughout these projects is the commitment to elevating the quality of life for many. Yet these projects also offer the opportunity to make their mark on their city's history. After all, the multifamily and mixed-use spaces will serve as homes and places of business for generations to follow.

Gables West Village, Looney Ricks Kiss Architects, Inc., page 64

Magnolia Hill, Architecture Demarest, page 76

Edgemere, Three, page 60

5225 Maple

Beeler Guest Owens Architects, LLP

As downtown neighborhoods undergo the revitalization process, the easiest sites are typically snatched up first. It takes the imagination of an artist and the patience of seasoned professionals to find the sometimes-hidden value in one of the last infill projects on a street and design beautiful architecture that takes advantage of its every square inch. For a uniquely shaped site on the 5200 block of Maple Avenue, formerly quite an industrial area, the architects of Beeler Guest Owens created an urban-chic multifamily residential structure that stretches from property line to property line. A diagonal axis visually expands the compact site on which a series of buildings encircle a luxuriantly landscaped courtyard and variety of amenity spaces.

FACING PAGE: Two parking structures and upwards of 200 units were skillfully woven into this dense, somewhat awkward piece of property to create a downtown residential community with overwhelming warmth.
Project Design Team: Jerry Beeler and Gary Pitts.
Photograph by Brian Barnaud

ABOVE LEFT: Reflective of the surrounding area's light industrial flavor, the monumental four-story atrium tower boasts large sheets of glass accentuated with stainless steel.
Photograph by Brian Barnaud

ABOVE RIGHT: A simple material palette of brick, metal and stained concrete informs the design's hard-loft character.
Photograph by Brian Barnaud

FACING PAGE LEFT: The arrangement of residential buildings creates a graciously sized courtyard—equally brilliant during the day and at night.
Photograph by Brian Barnaud

FACING PAGE RIGHT: Light infuses the space through the curvilinear glass-block wall. Steel ceiling trusses are left exposed in celebration of the architecture's materiality.
Photograph by Brian Barnaud

The firm's principals have made a habit of beginning each project by dreaming up a storyline that addresses the client's programmatic needs and goals. By committing 5225 Maple's story to paper, the architects were able to cling to the vision from concept to completion and ensure that every aspect, including curb appeal, material palette and the organization of interior spaces, bolstered the overall design. Inspiration was gleaned from the factory-like setting of the neighborhood in its earliest form. A steel factory next door gestured the architects to celebrate the materiality of metal, which they juxtaposed with earthen substances and large expanses of glass. Another nod to the industrial tone of the community transpires just before prospective residents tour the property. Guests are delightfully taken aback as a leasing agent situates a piece of paper and a template within the Heidelberg-like press and stamps floor plans right before their eyes. The architects created not only a unique living experience, but an exceptional home–seeking experience as well.

Beeler Guest Owens Architects' relationship with Carleton Developers spans more than three decades; when the latter expressed a desire that 5225 Maple cater to young professionals yet appeal to an even broader clientele, the architects responded with a variety of attractive lifestyle environments. Though all residences boast built-in casework, custom kitchen and bath components and open layouts, first-floor units have a hard-loft attitude with exposed mechanical elements, richly stained concrete floors and open layouts with moveable partitions, while upper units are carpeted, have more defined layouts and exude a soft-loft ambience.

The most successful projects are those in which the exterior architecture blends harmoniously with the interior. To ensure such continuity for the Maple project, the architects designed and specified everything from rooflines, handrails made of galvanized pipes and steel accent panels to exposed light bulbs, the layout of each unit and furniture placement in common areas. From the moment people make their way through the dual security gates and set foot in either the dramatic four-story, steel and glass information center or one of the 224 units, it simply feels like home. ■ ■ ■ ■ ■ ■ ■ ■ ■ ■ ■

The Ashton

■ ■

Gromatzky Dupree & Associates

■ ■ ■ ■ ■ ■ ■ ■ ■ ■ Swanking what is arguably the sexiest rooftop garden and pool deck in Dallas, and with more than half a dozen nationally sought-after design awards to its name, The Ashton represents more than luxurious uptown living; it defines a fresh urban lifestyle and sets a hard-to-surpass benchmark by which future architects will measure their success.

On the underpinning of having completed two wildly successful large-scale projects together—one in Houston, the other in Atlanta—The Hanover Company was delighted at the opportunity to work with Gromatzky Dupree & Associates to bring to fruition Cedar Springs Road's new landmark residential tower: The Ashton. The greatest potential hurdle of the project was earning the approval of owners of deeply rooted, nearby gems such as Crescent Court. However, upon seeing the proposed plan—with its sleek 21-story tower and pedestrian-scale five-story wing, not to mention the above-ground parking

FACING PAGE: The Ashton's richly detailed brick and cast stone exterior contributes to a sense of luxury and history, while also introducing contemporary elements.
Photograph by Ed LaCasse

area, brilliantly concealed within the main structure—endorsement was quick to follow.

Programmatically, The Ashton contains 663,000 square feet of prime living and socializing space; it is the prestigious address of more than 250 residents and families. A private screening room, library, business center, conference room, fitness center, clubhouse, climate-controlled wine cellar, state-of-the-art demonstration kitchen, outdoor café and mother-in-law suites—also suitable for out-of-town friends—are just a few of the draws. Because units are strictly available for lease, the architects were able to carry over the exterior's "soft Chicago contemporary" feel into the interior, which they accomplished through gracious 11-foot ceilings, exposed ductwork presented in an elegant manner, track lighting, beautifully stained wood floors, tall custom cabinetry, stainless-steel appliances and myriad other clean, rich finishes. Many of the residences have floor-to-ceiling glass to take in the downtown views and all have individualized entrances, lending a front-porch feel to the multifamily dwelling.

The Ashton is, in short, an architectural gem. Its high-rise portion ensures presence while the low-rise wing—clad with richly detailed brick and cast stone and bordered by wide sidewalks and thoughtful landscaping—creates amazing approachability for both pedestrian and motorist passersby. The signature breezeway entrance and low-rise wing's rounded termination further enhance The Ashton's sleek, unique, upscale essence. ■ ■ ■ ■ ■ ■ ■ ■ ■ ■ ■

TOP LEFT: Residential units conform to the soft-loft design, providing a homelike look with modern sensibility.
Photograph by Ed LaCasse

BOTTOM LEFT: Contemporary furnishings and materials in the lobby combine for a sophisticated environment in which residents may relax and unwind.
Photograph by Ed LaCasse

FACING PAGE: The Ashton's rooftop pool deck offers an infinity-edge pool and 180-degree views of downtown and the American Airlines Center.
Photograph by Ed LaCasse

CityHomes of Knox Park

Hensley Lamkin Rachel, Inc.

Designing one townhome community in a prominent Dallas neighborhood is a privilege, but when that project proves so successful that it spurs commissions for a dozen more within just a few blocks' radius, it becomes a special opportunity. Given creative freedom from Alan McDonald, the lead developer and owner of CityHomes, the architects of Hensley Lamkin Rachel, Inc. drew inspiration from the eclectic texture of the Knox Park neighborhood. This inspiration led to a series of distinctive, high-end residential communities.

Well versed in the challenges that accompany such projects, founding principals of Hensley Lamkin Rachel worked closely with the neighborhood committee to modify existing zoning guidelines. With a focus on revitalization and a sincere desire to have a positive impact on the neighborhood, the architects responded to the strict density requirements and the local special planning interests with traditional forms presented in a clean, urban

FACING PAGE: A modern archway frames the private drive of Elizabeth Square, where simple gable forms of brick, stucco and glass define townhome entrances. Photograph by Ira Montgomery

manner. This effort ensured that each infill project would fit contextually with the neighborhood yet make a statement of its own.

In addition, the respectful nature of the architects' relationship with CityHomes combined with CityHomes' ability to retain essentially the same team of consultants and subcontractors allowed projects to move swiftly and consistently attain a high level of quality.

The first undertaking, Elizabeth Square, displays a regional approach, with simple gable forms of brick and secondary areas of stucco and glass, which define entrances. Another three-story, Vitano, has a more modern architectural vocabulary. It offers greater density without compromising the privacy of its residents by featuring a semi-private courtyard and garden entry. A series of public and private spaces lead the owners from the street to the living space. A covered second-floor balcony runs the length of the home featuring large, storefront windows on the upper levels, which highlight two-story living spaces.

LEFT: Vitano features semi-private courtyards along Travis Street and dramatic two-story living areas.
Photograph by Doug Mandel

FACING PAGE LEFT: Morrison residents enjoy views of the Katy Trail with their third-story loft and front roof deck.
Photograph by Hensley Lamkin Rachel, Inc.

FACING PAGE RIGHT: Fontana utilizes glass and steel to create an industrial flare, and residents enjoy private, third-level rear roof decks.
Photograph by Mark Olsen

In designing the next project, Morrison, the architects carefully addressed the scale of the adjacent buildings along the street with a two-story brick façade stepping back to a third-story loft further off the street. The third-floor roof deck on the front orients the residents' view to the Katy Trail—a historic railway route turned pedestrian/bicycle path.

Hensley Lamkin Rachel also found inspiration in the traditional townhouse forms of eastern United States cities. Grammercy, for example, was inspired by the Federal style, prevalent in Washington, D.C., while Cambrick Square is reminiscent of Manhattan's stately brownstones with their simple, traditional residential forms and materials. Fontana, more modern in style with the industrial flare of glass and steel, boasts a combination of private yards or roof decks with access to a city park only a block away.

The principals of Hensley Lamkin Rachel design residential and mixed-use projects across the country but find exceptional joy in enhancing the architectural fabric of Dallas. Having three-dimensional portfolio pieces, such as the CityHomes projects, so close to their north Dallas design studio, allows them to demonstrate to associates and clients the caliber and quality of design that their firm's name represents. ■ ■ ■ ■ ■ ■ ■ ■ ■ ■ ■

Edgemere

■ ■

Three

■ ■ ■ ■ ■ ■ ■ ■ ■ ■ Nestled in the heart of north Dallas, near the city's most established and posh neighborhoods, is a continuing-care retirement community. It feels every bit like an 18th-century Tuscan village that has evolved over time, with its varied elevations, meandering stone walkways, lush landscaping mingled with water features, patinaed roof tiles, hand-mottled stucco walls and classical detailing. Edgemere's interiors are equally stunning as they are filled with intimate sitting areas and sprinkled with crackling fireplaces, vaulted ceilings, flowing fountains, paintings of idyllic countrysides and hand-blown Venetian glass.

A collaborative effort orchestrated by the professionals of Three, the thoughtfully designed five-star development caters to patrons with discriminating tastes, in various stages of retirement. With several hundred independent-living residences ranging in size from 800 to 1,500 square feet and assisted living

FACING PAGE: Tl e Tuscan-style reception court and porte cochere intimately welcome residents and guests alike to Dallas' preeminent retirement community.
Project Design Team: Rockland Berg, Carl S. Ede and Hunt Fugate.
Photograph by Grant E. Warner

and skilled nursing areas, couples have the luxury of residing together or in neighboring buildings as their needs change. The central spine organization ensures that those with less-vivid memories are able to easily find their way around the beautiful grounds. To further enhance the navigability, each building has distinct, asymmetrical massing and, depending on its function, is finished in any number of rich, earthen colors.

The master plan, conceived by Three and Greystone Communities, called for an assortment of amenities—a challenge that was overcome through careful calculating and a judicious allocation of resources. With the interests of retired Dallasites in mind, Edgemere was designed to include a myriad of common areas ranging from a library, coffee shop and cigar lounge to a greenhouse, spa, indoor pool, juice bar, fitness center, putting green, billiards room and performance center. Of course, the self-sufficient community also boasts a business center, salon and three fabulous dining rooms: a casual, vaulted sunroom with arched windows that overlooks the pond; a two-story space with a slightly more formal tone and a captain's table set within a cozy enclave; and a private, dimly lit dining room replete with an enchanting wine cellar.

As a whole, Edgemere represents the perfect marriage of modern amenities and Old World charm. The architects turned an area bustling with traffic into a quiet sanctuary of courtyards encircled by beautiful buildings. They took advantage of the 20-foot fall across the nearly 16-acre site by designing a

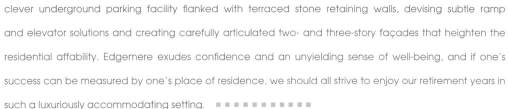

clever underground parking facility flanked with terraced stone retaining walls, devising subtle ramp and elevator solutions and creating carefully articulated two- and three-story façades that heighten the residential affability. Edgemere exudes confidence and an unyielding sense of well-being, and if one's success can be measured by one's place of residence, we should all strive to enjoy our retirement years in such a luxuriously accommodating setting. ■ ■ ■ ■ ■ ■ ■ ■ ■ ■ ■

ABOVE LEFT: Residents and their guests have direct access to Medici's fine dining and stunning décor featuring vaulted wood ceilings and rustic chandeliers.
Photograph by Grant E. Warner

ABOVE RIGHT: The state-of-the-art fitness and aquatics center fills with natural light, enhancing interaction with the outdoors.
Photograph by Grant E. Warner

FACING PAGE TOP: One of the many richly landscaped outdoor areas, the dining lagoon court is accented with water features enjoyed from both the stone walkways or balconies above.
Photograph by Grant E. Warner

FACING PAGE BOTTOM: The beautifully designed Henry S. Miller Performing Arts Theatre gives residents a place to enjoy educational seminars, lectures, movies and entertainment.
Photograph by Grant E. Warner

Gables West Village

■ ■

Looney Ricks Kiss Architects, Inc.

■ ■ ■ ■ ■ ■ ■ ■ ■ ■ ■ Doug Chestnut, President of Gables Residential, challenged Looney Ricks Kiss Architects with creating a vibrant, pedestrian-friendly mixed-use retail and residential project that blended into the urban fabric of Dallas' chic West Village district. LRK brought a wealth of mixed-use experience to this project, offering innovative solutions to challenges posed by the site's compact and urban nature.

With the initial phase of West Village's mixed-use district complete, Gables West Village was envisioned to further extend the success of the district. Working with a narrow city block—122 feet deep by 358 feet wide—the design team brought the building to the edge of the street, creating ground-level storefronts and a retail-friendly sidewalk environment. Gables West Village is comprised of 75 units over ground-floor retail. Responding to the site constraints, below-grade parking is provided for residents. Cars enter the garage mid-block between the two towers, and

FACING PAGE: Anchoring a vibrant corner in Dallas' West Village district, this Gables property offers an eclectic mix of residential, shopping and dining options.
Photograph by Steve Hinds Photography

a shared pool deck is elevated above the garage entrance. Shoppers are directed to surface area parking on the alley side of the building.

To attract the attention of future residents and shoppers, LRK created a bold architectural expression featuring classic building concepts accented by contemporary forms. With a transitional contemporary style, the building features a well-defined base of ground-level retail with four levels of loft-style residential living. The brick and stucco exterior is capped by a dramatic cornice, adding depth to the roof line, and metal and glass accentuate building edges for a contemporary expression.

The building is oriented such that it provides all residents with dynamic downtown views to the south. Loft-style apartment units feature the latest in contemporary residential design and finishes with open floor plans, elevated ceilings and floor-to-ceiling glass. An efficiently planned mixed-use development, Gables West Village anchors a vibrant yet densely packed neighborhood. ■ ■ ■ ■ ■ ■ ■ ■ ■ ■ ■

ABOVE LEFT: Metal elements add an "edgy" feel to brick and stucco exterior façades. Residents access below-grade parking via a convenient entrance beneath the elevated pool deck.
Photograph by Steve Hinds Photography

ABOVE RIGHT: Abundant large windows combine with a mix of balconies and patios to take advantage of spectacular downtown views.
Photograph by Steve Hinds Photography

FACING PAGE LEFT: The mid-block vehicular entrance leads to parking, and the elevated pool deck provides a valuable social space for residents along with dramatic views of the street scene.
Photograph by Steve Hinds Photography

FACING PAGE RIGHT: Street-level retail creates a pedestrian-friendly environment for residents and shoppers alike.
Photograph by Steve Hinds Photography

Lake Forest Urban Living Community
MESA

■ ■ ■ ■ ■ ■ ■ ■ ■ ■ ■ Just moments away from Dallas' major highway arteries lies Lake Forest Urban Living Community, a luxurious collection of private homes that transports its residents to another time and place, far from the city's hum and hurry. Hidden behind a stand of old-growth live oaks and an eight-foot-high, stone and wrought iron wall, the 64-acre neighborhood provides pastoral tranquility in a premium urban location.

To achieve this bucolic atmosphere, the project's developer, Republic Property Group Community, commissioned award-winning Dallas landscape architecture firm MESA to imbue the community with a distinct sense of place. Well known for its philosophy of balancing human needs with natural beauty in environmentally responsible, spiritually uplifting designs, MESA proved to be the ideal firm for the project. Though much of the land planning had been

FACING PAGE: Lushly landscaped, the main entry gateway on Hillcrest welcomes residents home.
Project Design Team: Stan Cowan, Robin McCaffrey and Fred Walters.
Photograph by Tom Jenkins

completed when the firm began design in 1994, lead project designers Stan Cowan and Fred Walters had a substantial vision for the project—to create a bold and romantic atmosphere that would remain beautiful and relevant for future generations.

Deeply sensitive to the fact that the project's impact would be twofold, the MESA team designed the project to resonate with residents and passersby, alike. Highly visible from well-traveled thoroughfares, the perimeter warranted careful planning. To set the tone for the neighborhood, the design team created an entrance evocative of an English countryside—a nod to the architecture of the homes within. The guardhouse evokes the residences in form, and both it and the screen wall spanning the perimeter are composed of Lueders Limestone, chosen for its rough texture and similar color to that of the Austin Chalk bed of the property's White Rock Creek.

As the land was home to numerous mature oaks, MESA consulted Houston's Environmental Design to evaluate and help relocate more than 60 old growth trees to the neighborhood's borders for all to enjoy. The firm also fought to keep the site's existing lake public, and it sits adjacent to the guard house, providing visitors a placid, welcoming image—a taste of the experience to come. Though many of the streets within the community had already been created, the MESA team redesigned their layout to dilute the vehicular movement, including larger landscaped clearings and cultivating a pedestrian, almost Olmstedian

atmosphere in the communal space. The drive is thus transformed into a romantic journey, one that encourages drivers to pause and enjoy the waterfalls and gardens around them without the need for stop signs. Moreover, the street system encourages cognitive mapping by the user, allowing pedestrians and motorists alike to intuitively understand the main path from the subordinate one as they move through the site.

At the time of construction, MESA's vision for Lake Forest's landscape was unique among gated communities. The quality and magnitude of the landscape that MESA was able to preserve and augment remained unmatched—anomalous, even—in other developments. Stan and Fred admit that shifting the subdivision paradigm involved a degree of risk; yet the rustic retreat they created within the city sprawl has proven well worth their efforts, and will for generations. ■ ■ ■ ■ ■ ■ ■ ■ ■ ■ ■

ABOVE LEFT: The lake is beautiful from every angle.
Photograph by Tom Jenkins

ABOVE RIGHT: Looking toward Hillcrest Road, mature trees are reflected in the lake.
Photograph by Tom Jenkins

FACING PAGE: An eastward view of the community reveals a waterfall just beyond the gatehouse of the main road.
Photograph by Tom Jenkins

Legacy Town Center

RTKL Associates, Inc.

■ ■ ■ ■ ■ ■ ■ ■ ■ ■ From the 1970s onward, Legacy Park blossomed as a burgeoning corporate corridor. Yet as the North Texas office park grew to a workforce population of 36,000 and became home to more than half a dozen industry giants' world headquarters, one thing became apparent: The area lacked a sense of place—and was devoid of commercial options that could service its sizeable daily population.

RTKL, an international planning, architecture and design firm involved in the success of hot spots like Dallas' State Thomas Historic District and Addison Circle, saw the potential in the site, and the firm was commissioned to create a 150-acre master plan that could transform it into a vibrant environment

FACING PAGE: Sensitive scaling, thoughtful adjacencies and an appropriate mix of uses generate a pedestrian-friendly environment that virtually eliminates the need for cars.
Photograph by Charles Davis Smith, AIA

enjoyed 24 hours a day. Today, the mixed-use community of residential, hotel, retail, restaurant and entertainment establishments has

emerged as a premier example of how urban planning and design can help to shape a vibrant and commercially viable community.

Why has the project been so successful? For one, Legacy Town Center is a place where people want to linger. In the creation of

the master plan, RTKL designers were careful to consider how every use, design element and streetscape component could form

a seamless framework of smart connections and visual harmony.

The pedestrian-friendly environment was accomplished by minimizing the presence of streets and maximizing the flow of traffic. Head-

in teaser parking facilitates quick access to the project's various uses and acts as a traffic-calming measure. Curbs project from each

corner so that pedestrians need only pass by two lanes of traffic, instead of two plus a row of parking on either side. The project's

ABOVE LEFT: Environmental graphics, public art, outdoor seating, landscaping and nighttime lighting create a dynamic streetscape.
Photograph by Charles Davis Smith, AIA

ABOVE RIGHT: Residential units located above ground-level retail and eateries create a buzz of activity and facilitate a sense of self-policing security.
Photograph by Charles Davis Smith, AIA

FACING PAGE TOP: Design elements that humanize the public appearance of the development strengthen its appeal as a unique live-work-play environment.
Photograph by David Whitcomb

FACING PAGE BOTTOM: Bishop Park serves as an urban "central park" with distinct entry points located along a low stone wall accented by stone portals and large ornamental urns.
Photograph by Charles Davis Smith, AIA

landscaping, which includes mature live oak trees harvested from Legacy Park, help to shape a relevant sense of place. Residential design elements, including balconies and porches, overlook the street and generate a buzz of activity.

The development's distinctive material palette was derived from North Texas' agricultural heritage: rich brown bricks were employed for the ground plane; clay and limestone were specified to complement the plaster and touches of masonry. As a nod to the original character of the land, a genuine water trough, made of corrugated metal, serves as a fountain for one of the multifamily residences' courtyards. The site's history is further reinforced along The Trails in Legacy, a collection of open-air sculptures that offers a glimpse into life on the Shawnee Trail in the late 19th century.

There is no shortage of things to see or do at Legacy Town Center, and the area's near-24/7 activity confirms it: the morning stir of residents out for a jog; the afternoon lunch rush of employees from the adjacent corporate campuses; and the early evening bustle of workers who linger to eat, dine and shop long after the workday is over. Quite simply: It's a place that works. ▪ ▪ ▪ ▪ ▪ ▪ ▪ ▪ ▪ ▪ ▪

Magnolia Hill

Architecture Demarest

■ ■ ■ ■ ■ ■ ■ ■ ■ ■ David Demarest, AIA, has a flair for designing gracious multifamily residences, skills learned from experiences undertaking such projects throughout the country and as far away as the Lan Zhou, Gansu Province of China. Closer to home, the original plan for the Magnolia Hill townhomes in downtown Dallas, presciently devised by David's firm, Architecture Demarest, has been an overwhelming success. The simple yet unique loft-style housing, along with its integration into the context of the district's historically significant, pre-existing architectural vernacular, give this community a sense of place and belonging.

FACING PAGE: The Magnolia Hill townhomes deftly incorporate the various brick patterns and colors from the industrial palette of nearby Magnolia Station in an innovative form.
Photograph by Steven Vaughan Photography

The area that is now home to Victory Park was quite different in 1995. It was home to the MKT railway lines, which later became the Katy Trail, a recycling center, a large abandoned grain silo, a public housing project and the Magnolia Station apartments, which were converted from the Magnolia Petroleum service center—hardly the most desirable location to build luxurious mid-rise town homes. David undertook the challenge of designing 20 industrial, loft-style town home residences nestled in this gritty, industrial neighborhood. David, already familiar with the area from previous design work on the West End Marketplace, Market-Ross Place and the Brewery, spent two-and-a-half years developing what would become a model and catalyst for the future development of Dallas' growing downtown residential community.

David's passion for historic renovation and adaptive reuse came into play from the onset. Cues were taken from the historic neighbor, Magnolia Station, incorporating its industrial style into the new lofts.

Architecture Demarest utilized a Victorian time frame and industrial-style thought process with the units, in addition to complementing various brick patterns and colors with the palette of Magnolia Station.

Inside, each three-story unit features steel frames, stained concrete floors and an infrastructure formed of heavy-tempered steel columns and beams protected by rust inhibitor, giving them a rich patina. Each unit's second-story, loft living area features two stories of glass, providing stunning views of the downtown Dallas skyline. The open third floor overlooks the living area, which affords spectacular downtown views, and incorporates industrial pine tongue-and-groove flooring. The units, all sold prior to the project's completion, have custom finish and styling throughout; owners worked with David to personalize and individualize their respective loft homes.

From this innovative construction design, with clever use of materials and interior floor plans, Architecture Demarest designed town homes that will endure, escaping association with any particular architectural style or time period—he refers to them as "100-year buildings." To illustrate this point, most of the original residents still call Magnolia Hill home.

From a property that was so unappealing David joked he thought his father would disown him if he undertook the Magnolia Hill project, to the push for what is now a downtown residential community rife with growth, Demarest's masterpiece not only succeeded, but has flourished and will undoubtedly stand the test of time. ■ ■ ■ ■ ■ ■ ■ ■ ■ ■ ■

ABOVE LEFT: Each unit has custom finishes and styling throughout; original residents worked closely with David to personalize their interior settings. Interiors by David Sterns.
Photograph by Steven Vaughan Photography

ABOVE RIGHT: The open third floor of these loft-style units overlooks the living area below and features industrial pine tongue-and-groove flooring. Interiors by Alice Cottrell Interior Design.
Photograph by Copyright Photography, Stephen Karlisch

FACING PAGE LEFT: The views of downtown Dallas from atop Magnolia Hill are simply sublime.
Photograph by Steven Vaughan Photography

FACING PAGE RIGHT: Each three-story unit is comprised of steel frames, stained concrete floors and an infrastructure formed of heavy-tempered steel columns and beams.
Photograph by Steven Vaughan Photography

Victory Park: The Terrace & The Vista

■ ■

WDG Architecture, Inc.

■ ■ ■ ■ ■ ■ ■ ■ ■ ■ WDG Architecture's cunning design and implementation of The Terrace condominiums and The Vista apartments at Victory Park—two of the first mixed-use residences in what is fast becoming the city's most desirable urban destination—effectively shaped a major component of this exciting development while granting an invaluable urban transition area between the historic West End District and Victory's northern anchor, the American Airlines Center.

While WDG had plenty of previous experience designing multifamily projects in mixed-use developments, The Terrace and The Vista residences presented an exciting opportunity to apply that knowledge in downtown Dallas. Utilizing a Texas contemporary architectural style, these structures provide a bridge between the more traditional style employed at the AAC and the modern approaches found at the W Hotel and other emerging projects at Victory.

FACING PAGE: The Terrace condominiums and Vista apartments were designed in a Texas contemporary style, which is characterized by a profusion of glass, limestone and brick.
Project Design Team: Jaime Fernandez-Duran, Vincent Hunter, Carl Maldonado and Walter Harry.
Photograph by Britt Stokes

Both residential buildings sit atop a first-floor retail base, which creates an active sidewalk environment that is further animated and integrated into the adjacent Victory Park.

This unique urban location presented WDG with the particular challenge of constructing buildings with essentially four front façades. Separately, parking, loading and service functions had to be constructed so as to not disrupt the heavy traffic flow that engenders this populated enclave. WDG's adept planning resulted in a logical loading and service solution that minimized the flow of traffic around the site while accommodating a forthcoming DART rail station. Constructed of the same limestone and exterior materials as the retail base, the service functions coalesce with the rest of the composition. Moreover, utilizing Houston Street's one-way nature, service functions are effectively screened in the direction of traffic and largely disappear from prominent views.

Collectively, The Terrace condominiums, The Vista apartments and their adjoining retail base serve as dynamic residences within a mixed-use urban development and an effective transition between Victory Park's disparate architectural styles—enabled by the skilled team at WDG Architecture. ■ ■ ■ ■ ■ ■ ■ ■ ■ ■ ■ ■

ABOVE LEFT: These mixed-use residences, some of the first in Victory Park, provide astounding views of nearby downtown Dallas.
Photograph by Britt Stokes

ABOVE RIGHT: Situated atop a first-floor retail base, vibrant retail shops create an active sidewalk environment that enriches the neighborhood context of The Terrace, foreground, and The Vista, background.
Photograph by Britt Stokes

FACING PAGE: The Terrace and Vista are the synthesis of two disparate styles: the traditional architectural vernacular comprising the historic West End and the more modern forms found throughout Victory Park.
Photograph by Britt Stokes

CHAPTER THREE
City Projects

Many city treasures are housed in public spaces, including libraries, churches, government buildings and educational facilities—or perhaps these buildings themselves are the treasures. The excitement a weekly trip to the public library or park evokes or the wonder a child feels stepping inside the cool interior of a museum surrounded by awe-inspiring works of art—these feelings are undeniably alive and guide the modern architects who commit their talents to these projects.

Whether the projects are entirely new, rehabilitative or for the purpose of historic preservation, there is a certain sense of grandeur and appropriateness that must be translated into the design plans—as is so eloquently exemplified in Prestonwood Baptist Church, designed by HH Architects, George Allen Senior Courthouse, extensively renovated by Rees Associates, and the City of Allen Public Library and Civic Auditorium, created by Pro-Forma Architecture. Public spaces must reflect the city and the contemporary attitudes of its inhabitants while parks must delicately integrate facilities and engaging aesthetics for all ages.

No city project is without its own set of challenges, yet those challenges offer the opportunity to create public buildings and spaces where knowledge, resources and enjoyment are readily available for everyone from the young to the elderly. Enjoy a look into what designers are developing for these city institutions and gain rare insight into their thoughts and inspirations for their city through these projects.

Dallas Area Rapid Transit Light Rail,
Hellmuth, Obata + Kassabaum (HOK), page 120

Oak Cliff Bible Fellowship Education Center, TGS Architects, page 136

Dominican Priory, Brown Reynolds Watford Architects, Inc., page 86

Dominican Priory

■■■■■■■■■■■■■■■■■■■■■■■■■■■■■■■■■■■■■■

Brown Reynolds Watford Architects, Inc.

■■■■■■■■■■■ The award-winning Dallas-based architecture firm of Brown Reynolds Watford Architects, known for its well-planned and aesthetically thoughtful educational, religious and governmental work, valued the unique challenge to design a new Priory—completed in 2002—as part of the exciting University of Dallas campus project.

The university decided that the school should expand northward along the ridgeline of the natural topography to accommodate future facility growth. However, the existing Priory, an aging accommodation and home to 15 Dominicans, lay in the path. The administration proposed to design and reconstruct the Priory to enhance the beauty of the campus and to afford the opportunity for a greater involvement of the friars in the campus community in exchange

FACING PAGE: Shadows from a nearby live oak tree are cast against stone, glass and copper, blending the natural elements with the man-made components of the building.
Photograph by Douglas S. Hankins, BRW

for the existing site. As a result of the dynamic nature of the Priory's dual purpose, the design of the building called for elements that made it both a comfortable personal residence for the Dominicans while also creating common areas to welcome frequent student visits.

For BRW's principal-in-charge, Craig Reynolds, FAIA, it was a most fitting project, as he had a long professional and personal history of proven respect for the architecture of the campus and its preservation. "It was a tremendous honor to work with the University of Dallas and also collaborate with the Dominicans. It was not just a project of which we are quite proud; it was an enriching experience to be exposed to a group of individuals who have dedicated their lives to serving those in their community." BRW Architects had designed the master plan for the campus, which largely included the late 1960s' designs of San Antonio architect O'Neil Ford. In addition, Craig had designed the renovations of several buildings on campus and was exceedingly familiar with the style and materials used. Gleaning inspiration from that knowledge, BRW set out to compose a new Dominican Priory that reflected the older architecture on campus.

With the overall design goal of the campus in mind, Craig used a holistic approach from site selection to material selection. The site was chosen partly based on Craig's intuition for what this, as of yet, intangible building would necessitate as well as the university's requirements. Craig says, "When considering the design of any building, among the most critical attributes which make a project unique to its intended use are its site and orientation." The steep hillside presented a continuous tree canopy and gradual slope, which now provides for

a glorious shaded path from the visitor parking to the front entry courtyard. This also created the area for the residents' parking under the building, minimizing the impact on the site. To accommodate the friars' wish to be near the campus yet remain distinct, the architects angled the building away from the campus but connected them by means of a meandering path that visitors enjoy as they stroll through the oak grove on their way to the chapel.

Although the contemporary building may appear to be in contrast to the centuries-old traditions of the Dominicans, the simplicity of the design complements a life of introspective prayer and respect for God's earthly gifts.

The building's material palette makes the most of the natural elements of stone, wood and copper and integrates complementary masonry materials used elsewhere on campus. While the copper and brick were influenced by the existing architectural design, one resounding difference in structure between the existing campus buildings and the new Priory is foundation.

The crowning glory and focal point of the Priory is the intimate chapel used for mass, daily reflection and prayer. A key design element for the chapel was the use of natural light, therefore the decision to have the facility overlooking a rolling green meadow and a forested hillside was ideal. The apertures to nature appear as colored glass windows drawing upon the varying hues of sunset skies and changing seasons. The ceiling of the chapel steps up with a series of light coves as the volume increases toward the altar, filling the space with a blend of natural and artificial light. Hand-troweled Venetian plaster glows with the infusion of light, providing a fitting backdrop to the crucifix commissioned for the chapel.

ABOVE: The public lobby faces northward, where interior materials flow into outdoor spaces beyond.
Photograph by Douglas S. Hankins, BRW

FACING PAGE: Hand-troweled Venetian plaster provides a fitting backdrop to the crucifix commissioned for the chapel while framed apertures provide controlled views of the live oak grove outside.
Photograph by Douglas S. Hankins, BRW

The Priory is clearly articulated as three components: private, common and public. The 14,000-square-foot facility consists of the chapel, a common activity room, a library, a large banquet-style dining room, a guest suite, 12 individual living quarters and a Prior's suite. Clerestory windows flood the residence corridor with natural light. The public lobby serves as a foyer to the chapel and to the friars' library day room. As with the Priory, and all of Craig's projects, each detail down to the furniture, is considered for a complete design. The interior wood accents complement and enrich its furnishings. "It is not unusual that our firm helps choose furnishings on many projects. I think people understand the value of our design team, who has an intimate grasp of the building in its entirety."

ABOVE LEFT: Custom-built furnishings and relics fit within the light-filled interiors of the chapel.
Photograph by Mark K. Olsen

ABOVE RIGHT: Refurbished doors from the campus' original priory building provide a warm texture against the cool slate and stone.
Photograph by Mark K. Olsen

FACING PAGE: The friars' residences are adjacent to the chapel.
Photograph by Mark K. Olsen

ABOVE: Nestled into a steep hillside, the new facility looks out over a rolling green meadow. The chapel's views are selective apertures reflecting on the shade trees, the meadow and the sky. The copper-clad wall of the chapel creates a warm contrast to the hues of the sky and landscape.
Photograph by Mark K. Olsen

LEFT: Each of the friars' residences includes a copper-faced study that projects outward from the masonry façade—a space for meditation.
Photograph by Douglas S. Hankins, BRW

FACING PAGE: Natural materials bathed in controlled natural light provide a calming effect within the lobby.
Photograph by Douglas S. Hankins, BRW

There is nothing inappropriate or ostentatious about the Priory; in its quiet simplicity it stands dignified and magnificent as a true testament to the all-encompassing role of architecture on its inhabitants, site and in achieving its ultimate goal. ▪ ▪ ▪ ▪ ▪ ▪ ▪ ▪ ▪ ▪ ▪

City of Allen Public Library and Civic Auditorium

■ ■

Pro·Forma Architecture, Inc.

■ ■ ■ ■ ■ ■ ■ ■ ■ ■ ■ In 2001, the city of Allen, needing a new library and wanting to spur long-term growth in its central business district, conducted an interview and design competition among select architectural firms—to design a dynamic library and adjoining civic auditorium as a catalyst for redevelopment of a progressive, multiuse downtown area. The city council unanimously selected Pro·Forma Architecture led by principal Jeff Bulla, a design-oriented firm with broad experience in large, complex projects. The resulting edifice is a 53,500-square-foot, highly functional, aesthetically pleasing facility that has become not only a unifying element for Allen, but also a destination unto itself.

FACING PAGE: A twilight view of the Allen Public Library reveals its dynamic civic presence and engaging personality.
Project Design Team: Jeff Bulla, Michael Archer, David Schall, Stephen Park, Rhoda Savage and David Searl.
Photograph by Craig D. Blackmon, FAIA

Pro·Forma, which already had previous experience with the city of Allen on a challenging vertical expansion of its police station—in addition to multiple other projects since then, has found their collaboration to be exceptionally favorable and mutually satisfying. The city of Allen had a vision for what it wanted for this prominent site—an engaging, dynamic civic presence—and by effectively imparting that vision to Jeff and his team, allowed them to realize those aspirations with the building's design.

To foster a sense of urban scale and anticipation, the facility was located to define the street edges and provide a sense of arrival. The exterior was designed to express two typically mutually exclusive typologies: establishing a sense of civic permanence while creating an exciting destination for the patrons. Brick and burnished concrete masonry lend an aura of permanence and monumentality, against which, metal was used to create excitement.

The patron services hall was clad with glass curtainwall, aluminum panels and perforated sunscreens to express its purpose and elliptical form. Metal panels in blue or gray wrap the cylindrical corner tower, sloped walls of the elevator, teen space, stair tower and coffee shop. Retail concepts including over-scaled signage, the corner tower, transparency and bookstore-style shelving create an exciting, patron-friendly atmosphere.

LEFT: The elliptical patron services hall is the heart of the library, with the check-out desk on the first floor and the reference desk above it on the second serving as focal and control points.
Photograph by Craig D. Blackmon, FAIA

FACING PAGE: Generous north and east glazing at both levels provides views out to the landscaped courtyard and offers a transparent, inviting face to arriving patrons.
Photograph by Craig D. Blackmon, FAIA

The library is zoned vertically so the first floor, home to the children's library, teen space, multimedia collections and other high-volume traffic areas, is the most active. The second level contains less-trafficked areas, though it is still highly functional and carefully tailored for specific uses: glass-fronted group study rooms; the reference, fiction and non-fiction collections; a computer lab, as well as individual computer stations; and a quiet reading room.

Age-specific spaces are a unique yet pragmatic element. For example, the entrance to the children's library is marked by a 400-gallon, see-through aquarium surrounded by "bubble" glass, and the adjoining room utilizes an aquatic theme with blue-green hues and cold cathode lighting.

A separate "Teen'scape" room offers middle and high school students a place geared toward their interests. Utilizing a teen focus group to ascertain what elements to incorporate, Pro·Forma designed a simple rectangular room, rotated in plan with one corner protruding through the exterior wall—replete with edgy pendant lights, black metal shelving with eggplant-colored end panels, a pair of lounge chairs with CD listening stations, low-sitting fabric-wrapped rocker chairs, four computer stations and a large, upholstered diner-style booth surrounding an amorphous-shaped table that functions as a flexible group study and social area.

The library also features such innovative elements as self-service checkout stations, an RFID materials circulation system, and a covered drive-thru lane providing access to both a book drop and a service window. A large courtyard in the center offers patrons a place to read or simply enjoy an open-air setting when the weather is agreeable. The courtyard also serves as a space to hold music or theatrical performances and other civic events.

However, the ideal location for a performance is undoubtedly the 290-seat civic auditorium—a tiered, multipurpose venue used for dance and music, plays, multimedia presentations, author visits,

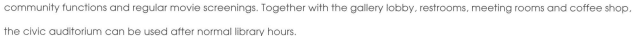

community functions and regular movie screenings. Together with the gallery lobby, restrooms, meeting rooms and coffee shop, the civic auditorium can be used after normal library hours.

All of these elements combine to collectively produce a compelling and enduring destination for the city of Allen, expressing the personality and character of the community while providing a highly functional, uplifting facility for its residents. The result is an active library with a steadily increasing membership that serves as a beacon to what the future holds for this progressive, growing city. ■ ■ ■ ■ ■ ■ ■ ■ ■ ■

ABOVE LEFT: The civic auditorium offers superb acoustics and features a radial seat layout with three descending box-seats that gradually reach stage level, providing full accessibility for the audience.
Photograph by Craig D. Blackmon, FAIA

ABOVE RIGHT: "Teen'scape" offers students a place geared toward their interests, so they not only feel comfortable within its confines, they feel a sense of ownership as well.
Photograph by Craig D. Blackmon, FAIA

FACING PAGE LEFT: The aquatic theme of the children's library is expressed through the fish-imprinted carpet, translucent wall panels, curvilinear shapes and fish cutouts in the furniture; fish designs even appear on the ceiling tiles.
Photograph by Craig D. Blackmon, FAIA

FACING PAGE RIGHT: To create an exciting, patron-friendly destination, the architects incorporated retail concepts such as over-scaled signage, a corner tower, transparency and bookstore-style shelving.
Photograph by Craig D. Blackmon, FAIA

El Centro College
Student & Technology Center Expansion

■ ■

CamargoCopeland Architects, LLP

■ ■ ■ ■ ■ ■ ■ ■ ■ ■ ■ The first college established as part of the Dallas County Community College District, El Centro College opened its doors in downtown Dallas in 1966, and for more than 40 years has offered a number of degree plans to local students intent on continuing their education. In 2002, when DCCCD decided to implement an expansion at its flagship campus, it was the PGAL/CamargoCopeland Architects team that was selected to embark upon the ensuing 32,000-square-foot, multilevel expansion and renovation that would help bring El Centro into the 21st century.

The El Centro expansion and renovation consisted of meeting the district's desire to create a new Student & Technology Center, while also amalgamating three separate, existing buildings to create a unifying "front door" entry element for the college. El Centro's location in the heart of downtown Dallas on Main Street made this project a unique challenge for PGAL/CamargoCopeland, as the style of the building expansion had to be compatible with the existing structures and be integrated seamlessly with the urban fabric of the area.

FACING PAGE: The new Student & Technology Center expansion defined a new entrance for DCCCD's flagship campus, responding to the urban context of the school. Photograph by Craig D. Blackmon, FAIA

Matching the style of the existing buildings to the new facilities proved to be a unique challenge, as the styles of the three buildings were exceptionally disparate—one of the buildings was a late-1800s' former department store clad in terracotta mosaic and very detailed, while a previous addition presented a simply detailed modern building designed by the late Enslie (Bud) Oglesby, a noted local architect. Being in the historic district of the West End—in addition to the building's listing on the National Register of Historic Places—PGAL/CamargoCopeland concluded that the best approach would be to harken back to the warehouse buildings and spaces that defined the area, using brick and cast stone to replicate the historic style of the area. The result was a bit of a compromise between the very intricate and the very simple, which was achieved by matching the existing brick while employing entirely different detailing.

To create the desired student activity center, PGAL/CamargoCopeland installed two rotundas, the bigger of which became the district's desired front door element. The smaller rotunda was skewed at an angle of approximately 60 degrees, which created new vertical circulation. The resulting ground-level space between the two rotundas then became the student center, and by creating a highly articulated

window wall façade, PGAL/CamargoCopeland created a positive-negative space that established a relationship to the sidewalk, and thus, the urban fabric.

The student center has been very well-received by El Centro students, who can be found utilizing the space on a daily basis. Moreover, the student center became the unifying element of the campus, in addition to becoming a circulation spine tying in the different facilities, connecting them horizontally and vertically. While the resulting ground level provided for student activities and included a lounge area, student art gallery, full-service cafe/snack bar and audio-video lounge, the upper level created

ABOVE: The student center provides a variety of comfortable study and seating arrangements, incorporating the latest technology through Wi-Fi internet connections in a calm but colorful setting.
Photograph by Craig D. Blackmon, FAIA

FACING PAGE: Open to the exterior for natural daylighting, the student center space also serves as the principal connector for three separate buildings, joining them as one.
Photograph by Craig D. Blackmon, FAIA

new space for student government offices and computer-training classrooms, providing the college its new Technology Center.

PGAL/CamargoCopeland had previously taken on projects involving educational facilities, but unlike those earlier endeavors, the El Centro expansion and renovation's location in Dallas' downtown district made nearly every aspect of design more complex. Further, the age of El Centro resulted in the facility having a lot of old structures and foundations for which there were no records. As such, while drilling for piers and completing other such structural tasks the project team was often met with unexpected obstacles. Compounding the intricacies of the project, there was a steady flow of traffic, and fire exit locations were constantly changing based on the circulation patterns because the project transpired during school sessions.

Despite the challenges of renovating and expanding an older building comprised of very different styles in a crowded urban environment, PGAL/CamargoCopeland effectively created a unifying front door for El Centro College, which created a circulation spine for the existing buildings, as well as the new Student & Technology Center. Pulling off an effective renovation amid such unique challenges speaks to the cunning architectural mastery employed by the team. ◼ ◼ ◼ ◼ ◼ ◼ ◼ ◼ ◼ ◼ ◼

TOP RIGHT: The expansion provides an urban plaza, maintaining important green space and emphasizing its role as a connector.
Photograph by Craig D. Blackmon, FAIA

BOTTOM RIGHT: El Centro's new front door is equally as welcoming to evening students as it is during the day.
Photograph by Craig D. Blackmon, FAIA

FACING PAGE LEFT: Rotunda elements used as an anchor provide a sense of entry, responding to the context of the surrounding historic district.
Photograph by Craig D. Blackmon, FAIA

FACING PAGE RIGHT: The interior entry rotunda space provides quiet study areas and enables the historic district context to become evident.
Photograph by Craig D. Blackmon, FAIA

George Allen Sr. Courthouse

Rees Associates, Inc.

■ ■ ■ ■ ■ ■ ■ ■ ■ ■ ■ Texas has a long history of constructing architecturally significant county courthouses. The recently expanded and renovated George Allen Sr. Courthouse, originally built in the mid-1960s, has now joined the ranks of these proud structures. Few architects are fortunate enough to be commissioned to design a major public building in the heart of one of the most prominent cities in America. The architects and designers of REES were afforded this rare opportunity and made the best of it.

Meticulous research, planning, design and thoughtful attention to detail led to the spectacular re-emergence of the George Allen Sr. Courthouse and its rightful place in the heart of Dallas. This building effectively consolidates Dallas County Civil Court departments and functions into a previously

FACING PAGE: The 182,000-square-foot addition was blended into the existing 430,000-square-foot structure, which now houses all of Dallas County's civil courts.
Project Design Team: Robert Boyle, Jan Blackmon, Lance Braht, Linda Bernauer, Bari Larsen, Glen Redmond and Kelly Giddens.
Photograph by Craig D. Blackmon, FAIA

nondescript half-century-old building—transforming the structure into a monument of stability and civic pride for one of America's foremost cities. This was accomplished while juggling extreme site limitations and a modest construction budget.

Robert Boyle, AIA, led the REES architectural team from project conception to completion. To ensure the building's timelessness, the architectural team went to great lengths to match the existing marble used on the exterior of the original building. This unique white marble was traced to a Vermont quarry that had been closed for decades. The quarry, now owned by a stone processing company located in Pietrasanta, Italy, agreed to reopen and provide enough marble to complete the new court tower. The marble was quarried in Vermont, cut and prepared in Italy, and shipped to Dallas for the George Allen Sr. Courthouse—the result is a perfect match.

The George Allen Sr. Courthouse now has an immediately recognized entry accessible from both street level and a newly expanded underground parking garage. The grand lobby, with tastefully integrated

security screening checkpoints, enables visitors to efficiently and quickly enter the courthouse from a single location, resulting in an overall safer court environment.

The building's vertical expansion and horizontal renovation enabled the designers to increase critically needed staff work areas while simultaneously reducing visitor congestion in the existing court corridors. To maximize elevator efficiency, courts with the highest visitor volumes were relocated to lower floor levels. Escalators also serve these high-volume floors, further enhancing vertical movement of visitors using the building.

ABOVE LEFT: The grand lobby is both welcoming and secure.
Photograph by Craig D. Blackmon, FAIA

ABOVE RIGHT: Like its 16 virtually identical counterparts, this courtroom has durable beech wood surfaces and soft, off-white walls. The witness stand can be positioned on either side of the judge or directly across from the jury.
Photograph by Craig D. Blackmon, FAIA

FACING PAGE: Natural light eases lingering apprehensions as people await their time in court.
Photograph by Craig D. Blackmon, FAIA

The REES team of professionals, working closely with members of the court, was able to create a flexible courtroom layout capable of meeting the needs of multiple civil court jurisdictions. All but one of the new courtrooms are identical—ideal from a cost-savings perspective. One large ceremonial courtroom has been provided that is capable of serving large multilitigate trials as well as appellate court hearings. Throughout the building and courtrooms, special attention was paid to sight lines, acoustics and lighting, imperative elements of design for a courthouse.

Fully appreciating the George Allen Sr. Courthouse renovation and addition as a once-in-a-lifetime opportunity, the architects of REES put their hearts and souls into this building, and through their inventiveness and attention to detail they created a legacy that will decidedly stand the test of time. ■ ■ ■ ■ ■ ■ ■ ■ ■ ■

ABOVE: A sculptural element, the sweeping roof canopy—which runs the length of the building—seamlessly marries the original structure with the addition, creating the illusion that the building has always been a full 12 stories and that it was designed expressly for the site. At night, each pane of glass sparkles like a piece of crystal, softly illuminating the adjacent parks.
Photograph by Craig D. Blackmon, FAIA

FACING PAGE LEFT: The ceremonial courtroom is the largest of 18 yet maintains the same superb acoustics and sight lines.
Photograph by Craig D. Blackmon, FAIA

FACING PAGE RIGHT: George Allen Sr. Courthouse is beautifully blended into its downtown site.
Photograph by Craig D. Blackmon, FAIA

Addison Athletic Club

Ron Hobbs Architects

■■■■■■■■■■ Outdoor pools are typically enjoyed for a mere three months out of every year, but when Ron Hobbs and his team were commissioned to transform the Addison Athletic Club into a chic neighborhood gathering place that matched the vibrancy of the city, he envisioned the pool as a recreation area as well as a focal point—a sculptural element that could be enjoyed inside as well as outside, all year long.

The architects began the threefold undertaking of expanding the athletic club, creating a pool and integrating a park by absorbing the ideas and concerns of the users through the citizens' advisory committee. Some were worried about the overall impact the building would have on the community

FACING PAGE: Second-floor fitness rooms overlook the swimming pool. The cabanas are seemingly carved from the base of the building to provide shelter from the sun.
Project Design Team: Ron Hobbs, Kathy Thompson, Wadona Stich and David Tobin.
Photograph by Derwin Broughton

ABOVE LEFT: The aquatic center combines swimming pools with a variety of water features.
Photograph by Ron Hobbs

ABOVE RIGHT: The building's design affords privacy for the pool area while buffering the adjoining neighborhood from outdoor activities.
Photograph courtesy of the City of Addison

FACING PAGE TOP: At night, the building stays lively with its interesting transparency.
Photograph by Derwin Broughton

FACING PAGE BOTTOM: The large, second-floor fitness room is a series of interconnected modules, the smaller of which provide users with privacy.
Photograph by Wadona Stich

and felt that the lighting, increased traffic and pool area noise would disturb the peace, while others—like a woman who wanted the workout space to have niches that would afford privacy, and those patrons who requested higher quantities of the most-used equipment—had more personal concerns; all potential issues were taken into account and seamlessly surmounted.

Starting with the sweeping circle of the parking area, a curvilinear, colonnaded path leads patrons along the lower level of the pool, and as it meets the building, the pool curves back like a mirror image, creating visual interest and movement. Cleverly nestled into a large triangular niche, the pool is visible from many locations—most importantly, through the floor-to-ceiling windows of the exercise space above. Replete with upscale water features, the multilevel pool is filled by a three-foot waterfall at the deepest and highest point; subsequent aqueducts transfer the water downward, concluding with a zero-depth children's entry.

As Ron Hobbs Architects is mindful to marry elements of architecture and interior design, Addison Athletic Club's interiors are just as stunning as the beautifully scaled exterior. A timeless palette of materials bolstered the design continuity, so as patrons make their way to the considerably expanded and entirely redesigned exercise room they are welcomed by cool, refreshing blues and grays, a profusion of natural light and interesting circle motifs, which are repeated on the ceiling and floor to exude the energy of a successful workout. Amenities are plentiful, yet it is the intangibles—its timelessness, inviting and energetic ambience and ability to appeal to the community's broad demographic of families, young professionals and retired folks, alike— that make Addison Athletic Club truly spectacular. ■ ■ ■ ■ ■ ■ ■ ■ ■ ■

Allen City Hall

■ ■

Ron Hobbs Architects

■ ■ ■ ■ ■ ■ ■ ■ ■ ■ ■ The centerpiece of the Dallas suburb's master-planned civic center complex and an icon of the city as a whole, Allen City Hall looks as though it grew from the very ground on which it stands. Inspired by the city's geographical uniqueness—with its prevalent creeks teeming with stratified limestone—architect Ron Hobbs, who has thoroughly studied Allen's history and analyzed its future, designed the building and specified that it be crafted primarily of regionally quarried limestone and glass, a pleasant textural juxtaposition of timeless materials.

Massive five-foot-long by 30-inch-tall slabs of richly colored "roughback" limestone line the building's base; atop the slabs, more refined, honed-surface limestone—in 30-inch by 15-inch blocks—is situated. The material specification combined with the sweeping shape of the building creates visual interest,

as does the water sculpture, which was designed in collaboration with Brad Goldberg, an internationally acclaimed local artist who specializes in limestone. Every element, from the water—which flows in the direction of the building—to the natural curves of the landscaping and even the spiral-like shape of Allen City Hall itself, directs attention to the central rotunda.

Aesthetically, Allen City Hall is exquisite, but the organization of spaces and broad-reaching flexibility of function that it affords are, perhaps, its most significant attributes. When the civic center master plan was developed in the mid-1980s—incidentally, by a close friend and colleague of Ron's—what was considered adequate space for a 20,000-square-foot building was allocated; however, two decades later, the city's needs had substantially increased and the city hall evolved into a 65,000-square-foot design, carefully blended into an expanded yet still challengingly compact site. To the given set of programmatic and site parameters, the professionals of Ron Hobbs Architects responded with a four-story design, the bottom floor being mostly below grade.

The architects and city officials, alike, saw the project as an opportunity to capture the essence of Allen and demonstrate it to the public. The grand rotunda welcomes all to enter—whether or not they have official business to

conduct—since it serves as a gathering space for varied civic and private functions. Unlike city halls of yesteryear, Allen's premier space is easy to navigate as the most frequented spaces are smartly located nearest the main entry, and citizens in need of visiting several departments are delighted to find that the architects understood their needs and consolidated related activities, all of which are located off the main rotunda. This affords convenience for visitors and increased privacy for city staff members whose offices are located furthest in length and height from the public area.

Ron Hobbs Architects' design philosophy has long been that a successful building is one that expresses its purpose and the attitude of its users and is harmoniously married to its site. Allen City Hall would not make sense anywhere else, and its site felt empty without it. ■ ■ ■ ■ ■ ■ ■ ■ ■ ■

ABOVE LEFT: An identifiable civic icon, the cylindrical atrium is both an architectural element of interest and a point of welcome.
Photograph by Wadona Stich

ABOVE RIGHT: Public spaces and employee work areas are smartly oriented around the central atrium space.
Photograph by Jack Weigler

FACING PAGE: Relating, even responding, to its site, the building rises from a natural, exposed limestone shelf.
Photograph by Wadona Stich

Dallas Area Rapid Transit Light Rail

■ ■

Hellmuth, Obata + Kassabaum (HOK)

■ ■ ■ ■ ■ ■ ■ ■ ■ ■ From the time the city of Dallas first considered a high-speed light rail system in the early 1980s to when commuter services began in June 1996, DART weathered a failed bond election, construction delays, nine pull-out votes and financial concerns before opening the 20-mile starter system on time and budget. It was the prescient planning and sagacious design from the accomplished team at HOK that laid the groundwork for what was the first light rail system in both Texas and the Southwest, and is one of the top-10 most-used light rail systems by ridership in the United States.

Early on, HOK assessed station locations along three light rail thoroughfares regarding potential vehicular circulation, pedestrian linkages into neighborhoods, bus access points and potential issues relevant to specific neighborhoods. The project team devised conceptual site plans for all

FACING PAGE: A DART light rail train pulls into the Cedars Station at dusk. HOK designed the station prototype that was implemented at all light rail stations.
Project Design Team: Kirk Millican, Linda Bernauer, Mark Bowers and Farzine Hakimi.
Photograph by Craig D. Blackmon, FAIA

stations, in addition to studying corridor land-use plans and joint development opportunities, and facilitated community involvement meetings for station neighborhoods. The final site selections for the 20-mile starter system were chosen from HOK's invaluable counsel.

Establishing a prototype from which the original 14 light rail stations were forged, HOK formulated the design standards, criteria and drawings that were implemented across all stations. Evoking the historical train stations of Western Europe and early 20th-century American inner-urban stations, HOK designed four arcaded canopies that extend the length of the tracks from platform to platform; each station is outfitted with nearly 300-foot-long, low-level platforms. The grandiose canopies procure a distinct sense of entrance and departure at each station, as well as foment a discernible feeling of destination within each neighborhood.

While HOK's station prototype was adapted by other architects for construction purposes—albeit each station was carefully reviewed for conformance to the project team's standard and directive drawings—HOK completed final design and construction documents for three light rail stations. Two of those stations are located at the Dallas Convention Center and Union Station, which is an intermodal station connecting DART's light rail, commuter rail and bus services with Amtrak's inter-city service.

HOK also designed the Cedars Station, the light rail's first stop heading south from downtown Dallas and the convention center. Reflective of its diverse neighborhood, the Cedars Station borders against a parking garage, the

adjacent wall of which is covered with cement plaster and ivy, establishing a green, "living" wall as the station's backdrop. Four arched, steel-truss canopies are joined over the station's tracks by a metal roof span, affording valuable weather protection. Moreover, the canopies are comprised of silver metallic roofs and columns adorned with polished, architectural concrete panels and stainless steel attachments, providing a stark contrast between the green garage wall and the canopies' machine aesthetic.

Vastly exceeding all expectations, DART and HOK were recognized in 2000 by the U.S. Department of Transportation with a Design for Transportation National Honor Award. ▪ ▪ ▪ ▪ ▪ ▪ ▪ ▪ ▪ ▪ ▪

ABOVE LEFT: The stations' grand canopies are defining elements, engendering a discernible sense of arrival and departure while creating a semblance of destination within each neighborhood.
Photograph by Craig D. Blackmon, FAIA

ABOVE RIGHT: Union Station, highly functional and widely used, is an intermodal station connecting DART's light rail, commuter rail and bus services with Amtrak's inner-city service.
Photograph by Craig D. Blackmon, FAIA

FACING PAGE: The Cedars light rail station, the train's first stop heading south from downtown, is characterized by its vaulted metal canopies, pre-cast concrete column covers and steel-and-glass wind screens.
Photograph by Craig D. Blackmon, FAIA

Granbury City Hall

Randall Scott Architects, Inc.

The city of Granbury has a rich history dating back to the 1850s with pristine examples of historic downtown Texas architecture such as the 1886 Granbury Opera House and the 1888 Hood County Courthouse. In 2000, the city, which derives the majority of its tax revenue from tourism, voted to construct a new city hall. The new municipal facility was slated to house city administration, public service counters, a municipal court, the police department, council chambers and a visitor's center. The city tasked Randall Scott Architects, a firm respected throughout Texas for designing contextually appropriate municipal architecture, with creating a historically relevant building befitting Granbury's historical context.

FACING PAGE: Granbury City Hall's exterior is defined by its large limestone blocks, wood cornices and eloquent soffit panels painted with a historic palette of burgundy, rose and olive green.
Project Design Team: Randall B. Scott and Gregory J. Conaway.
Photograph by Carolyn Brown

The siting and shape of the new city hall were influenced by the owners' desire to remain in their existing city hall on site until the new building was completed and the presence of an estuary of Lake Granbury to the north. Randall Scott Architects' design called for a long, slender two-story limestone-clad building with large wood windows overlooking the estuary to the north and an extensive civic plaza leading up to the stately structure from the south.

Referencing the historic vernacular embodied in Granbury's opera house and courthouse on the square, the city hall's exterior is fashioned of large limestone blocks with generous wood cornices and articulate soffit panels painted with a historic palette of rose, burgundy and olive green. The prime architect, Randall Scott Architects, in conjunction with associate firm Larson and Pedigo Architects, preserved the site's mature oaks, adding to the site's historic character.

Patrons to the city hall are welcomed into the two-story 1,200-square-foot lobby appointed with rustic limestone walls, inlaid Brazilian mesquite wood floors, stamped metal ceilings and copper service counters, all of which overlook a fountain in the estuary to the north through generous wood windows. The warmth of the rustic Brazillian mesquite wood floor stands in sharp contrast to the stamped tin ceiling, which is a prevelent feature in Granbury's downtown historic structures. The second floor of the lobby leads to archway-covered balconies overlooking the estuary and plaza.

The council chambers on the second floor are an appropriate civic space, handsomely appointed with American cherry paneling, golden-colored woven fabric, silver-stamped metal ceiling panels and carpeted floors. The council chambers were designed by Randall Scott Architects to function as a municipal court by day and council chambers by night. Conceived as a grand historic meeting area for civic and other public assemblies, the space has state-of-the-art audio/visual capabilities replete with an 80-square-foot rear projection screen for citizens to view exhibits; flat-screen monitors for each council member at the dais; full connectivity for council, staff and press; and television broadcasting/recording capabilities.

Designing a contextually germane building with modern technologies, Randall Scott Architects achieved an astute civic solution for the Granbury City Hall by creating a sophisticated, enduring facility that expanded the city's downtown historic district while celebrating the city's rich architectural heritage. ■ ■ ■ ■ ■ ■ ■ ■ ■ ■

ABOVE LEFT: The two-story entrance lobby has rustic limestone walls and imported Brazilian mesquite wood floors.
Photograph by Carolyn Brown

ABOVE RIGHT: A detail view of the historic replica stair balustrade with cherry wood cap and handrail.
Photograph by Carolyn Brown

FACING PAGE: The council dais is appointed in American cherry and features an authentic stamped metal ceiling.
Photograph by Carolyn Brown

Ismaili Jamatkhana

■■■■■■■■■■ ■

Hidell & Associates Architects, Inc.

■■■■■■■■■■ "The Center will be a place of peace, humility, reflection and prayer... It will be a center which will seek to bond men and women of this pluralist country, to replace their fragility in their narrow spheres by the strength of civilized society bound together by a common destiny."

– His Highness the Aga Khan, 49th hereditary Imam of the Ismaili Muslims, at the opening of the Ismaili Jamatkhana, in Sugar Land, Texas, 2002.

Commissioned in 2004 by IMARA Development Services to design and build a new Jamatkhana for the Plano Ismaili community, Hidell & Associates Architects designed this house of worship and community center.

FACING PAGE: Illuminated, covered walkways etched with interlocking octagons and hand-painted tiles surround a tranquil fountain, which creates a tone of calm reflection at the entry.
Photograph by Patrick Coulie

Bill Hidell brought a keen awareness of Islamic architecture gleaned from his time spent among the historic palaces, mosques and Char Baghs of captivating Isfahan, Iran. This new enduring facility infuses the transcendent qualities of Islamic architecture with modern aesthetics, facilitating cultural and social interaction in a harmonious setting.

Islamic design is predicated largely on symmetry of form and ruled by geometry. The architects selected a simple geometric pattern on which to base the facility's design—a square, rotated to arrive at interlocking octagons, the genesis for the design that permeates the facility. Set on a serene eight-acre tract in Plano, the Jamatkhana addresses the Qibla, or Mecca, while vehicular traffic is shielded outward toward the perimeter, creating an oasis of green that eschews the hurried nature of modernity.

Entering the Jamatkhana, a serene space replaces the rush of daily life. A tone of calm reflection and humility imbues the path from the front lawn up to the luminous façade of the front entry. The immaculate glass wall fronts the social lobby area—its transparency serving as an acknowledgement of this pertinent space. Always a welcoming beacon to the community, the lobby glows at night yet remains lucid during the day.

Inside the social lobby, metal panels etched with rotated squares create an evolving pattern of light and shadow onto the interlocking octagons configured in the floor. The social lobby, centrally planned as two interlocking octagons,

ABOVE LEFT: Metal panels etched with rotated squares create an evolving pattern of light and shadow within the interior of the social lobby.
Photograph by Patrick Coulie

ABOVE RIGHT: The social lobby is defined by its voluminous octagonal shape, interlocking patterned floor, ornamental wood benches and lights and sculpted metal screens located on the columns.
Photograph by Patrick Coulie

FACING PAGE: Transparent glass walls signify a beacon to the community and a backdrop to the decorative, metallic screens depicting a fusion between history and contemporary.
Photograph by Patrick Coulie

gently orientates congregants toward the Prayer Hall. Approaching the Prayer Hall, the geometry becomes more structured, its patterns—delineated through wood, copper and stained glass on the walls, ceiling and floors—create a unity and calmness of space. Impeccably conceptualized and actualized, the geometric motif encapsulates all ceiling, wall and lighting designs in three-dimensional form, mirroring their two-dimensional equivalents on the floor.

The formal, exterior garden area, or Char Bagh, symbolizes Paradise on Earth, and is replete with a tranquil fountain and aromatic flora, which create a sublime setting for quiet contemplation or community fellowship.

The Jamatkhana in Plano has fulfilled the aspirations of the Ismaili community and gives an eclectic destination to the city of Plano. ■ ■ ■ ■ ■ ■ ■ ■ ■ ■ ■

Lake Pointe Church's Pier 4:19

HH Architects

Having completed several projects for Rockwall's Lake Pointe Church over the years and built a strong working relationship in the process, the professionals of HH Architects were excited at the prospect of designing a youth building for the growing congregation. Its endearing appellation, Pier 4:19—referring to the Biblical passage in Matthew in which Jesus says, "Follow me, and I will make you fishers of men"—is evangelistic in nature and suggests that special things are happening behind its intriguing, custom tilt-wall façade.

With multifaceted programmatic requirements ranging from a student worship auditorium and classrooms to a variety of hangout spaces, a café and both indoor and outdoor sports facilities, an architecturally eclectic flavor seemed appropriate. The architects specified an interesting combination of

FACING PAGE: Because architecture as eclectic as Lake Pointe's could have been perceived as out of place in the suburban setting, the exterior façades were carefully married with the adjacent styles of buildings. One side has a whimsical look, which relates to the shopping center it faces, while the other is clad in repurposed metal siding, a nod to the nearby dock.
Photograph by Edmonson Photography Studio

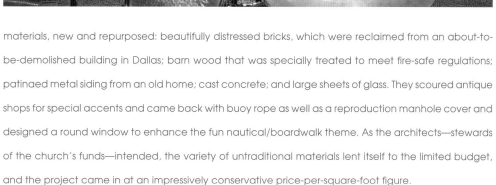

materials, new and repurposed: beautifully distressed bricks, which were reclaimed from an about-to-be-demolished building in Dallas; barn wood that was specially treated to meet fire-safe regulations; patinaed metal siding from an old home; cast concrete; and large sheets of glass. They scoured antique shops for special accents and came back with buoy rope as well as a reproduction manhole cover and designed a round window to enhance the fun nautical/boardwalk theme. As the architects—stewards of the church's funds—intended, the variety of untraditional materials lent itself to the limited budget, and the project came in at an impressively conservative price-per-square-foot figure.

Worship is the primary function of Pier 4:19, and the building's auditorium, which seats 600 and can expand to accommodate 300 more, is outfitted with the ultimate in audio-visual equipment, yet pastors and youth, alike, appreciate the broad flexibility of the cleverly laid-out space. In the main common area, two stacked basketball cages house games of three-on-three, making spectatorship stimulating to say the least. In keeping with the dock theme, the outdoor area features a sand volleyball court and

an inline skate park, the presence of which inspired a pastor—now endearingly referred to as "the Skate Pastor"—to start a new ministry that reaches a previously untapped congregation.

The effects of Pier 4:19 have been profound. Upwards of 1,000 youth attended the inaugural service and there were more than 150 decisions for Christ that very day—an unmatched return on investment. The continued increase in youth activity has created an explosion in the general congregation's attendance as each member of the family now has a dedicated place to fellowship and worship. ▪ ▪ ▪ ▪ ▪ ▪ ▪ ▪ ▪ ▪ ▪

ABOVE LEFT: Though the theater is impressive in size, its thoughtful design affords an intimate feel.
Photograph by Shands Photography

ABOVE RIGHT: Stacked three-on-three basketball cages serve as the focal point of the indoor youth hang-out areas.
Photograph by Shands Photography

FACING PAGE: The youth auditorium's flexible design allows expansion to up to 900 seats.
Photograph by Edmonson Photography Studio

Oak Cliff Bible Fellowship Education Center

■ ■

TGS Architects

■ ■ ■ ■ ■ ■ ■ ■ ■ ■ "We just came from the dedication of the Education and Youth Center. If you haven't been there yet, you need to go take a look. It's impressive. The brick and mortar is impressive. The architectural design is fantastic. What's more fantastic is what's going to take place inside the building." – President George W. Bush, Oak Cliff Bible Fellowship Education Center, October 2003.

Experiencing rapid growth and needing new K-12 education facilities, Oak Cliff Bible Fellowship envisioned a dynamic education center that would provide a unique and vibrant place not only for its students, but its congregation and the rest of the community. Commissioning TGS Architects to develop a comprehensive master plan and design for the new 170,000-square-foot, two-story private education facility, the progressive-minded firm fused education and entertainment using contemporary forms in a way that provided an engaging, enduring solution to the church's needs.

FACING PAGE: A delicate balance of stone and glass characterizes the compelling façade of the main gymnasium's glass wall exterior.
Project Design Team: Bill Ward, Dallas Taylor, John Pizzarello and Amy Renno.
Photograph by Mark Olsen

In addition to the education center's customary 54 classrooms and library space, the facility is replete with high-end entertainment, athletic, music and multipurpose areas. Desiring superior athletic facilities to host a basketball league featuring athletes from all over the city, not just church leagues, TGS implemented a state-of-the-art gymnasium complex covered with a green metallic barrel vault and glass walls at the ends, introducing outside light into this sporting area. The athletic facilities are further enhanced by an indoor running track and dual locker rooms with showers.

A nearby youth center for middle- and high-school students also aims to provide students with exceptional amenities to ensure their enjoyment. Upon running into the youth center through a large canopy and billowing smoke—much like a football team charging onto the field through its locker room—students are met by copious plasma-screen televisions, a game room, video wall, stage for music performances, soundproof music practice rooms and a coffee bar, which was originally planned as a bowling alley.

ABOVE LEFT: A highly detailed, stained concrete floor reflects the light washing down from the continuous, barrel-vaulted roofing system in this gathering space.
Photograph by Mark Olsen

ABOVE RIGHT: A pronounced canopy bathes the largely glass exterior of the Nigat entry in light, creating an engaging access point.
Photograph by Mark Olsen

FACING PAGE TOP: Warm yet durable red brick is accented by green metal window frames.
Photograph by Mark Olsen

FACING PAGE BOTTOM: The first-class gymnasium features an indoor running track looking over the basketball court, which is used by basketball leagues comprised of players from all across Dallas.
Photograph by Mark Olsen

The facility is designed around a central courtyard, which provides garden space and a secure play environment for kids while also filtering daylight into interior rooms. The exterior of the facility is comprised of warm yet durable brick and stone, accented with green metal window frames and a continuous barrel-vaulted metal roofing system. Interior spaces include a highly detailed, stained concrete floor throughout the atrium and gathering space, and are highlighted by natural stone and additional natural light introduced through a clerestory system ingrained into the barrel vault.

A dramatic yet graceful edifice fulfilling Oak Cliff Bible Fellowship's pertinent need for a highly functional education facility, TGS Architects' adroit planning and design produced the consummate solution to the church's unique needs. ▪ ▪ ▪ ▪ ▪ ▪ ▪ ▪ ▪ ▪

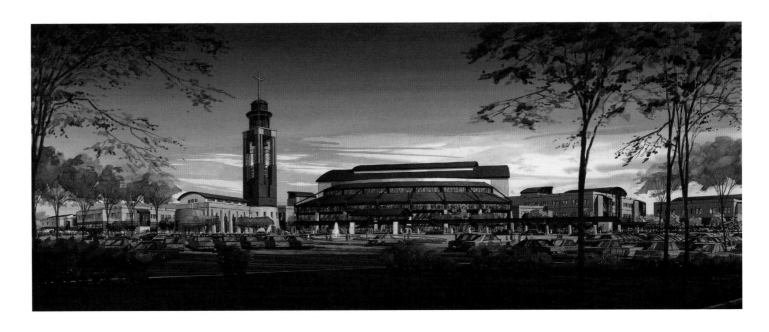

Prestonwood Baptist Church

HH Architects

■ ■ ■ ■ ■ ■ ■ ■ ■ ■ While the founder of HH Architects, Jerry Halcomb, did not originally set out to specialize in ecclesiastical building design, he is certainly glad it worked out that way. He lightheartedly refers to being selected in the early 1970s—before "megachurches" achieved widespread popularity—to design some of the nation's largest churches as "a God thing" that set him on the path to doing this work.

Jerry's relationship with Prestonwood Baptist Church's venerated pastor, Dr. Jack Graham, reaches back a number of years, as the two first worked together in Oklahoma, shortly after Pastor Graham graduated from seminary. The project took root in the mid-1990s when Prestonwood's increasing

ABOVE: The worship center's master plan echoes the character of the congregation.
Rendering by Bill Hendricks Delineator

FACING PAGE: At sunset, the stained glass window panels—each depicting a book of the Bible—are particularly exquisite.
Photograph by Dave Edmonson, Edmonson Photography Studio

attendance and limited parking mandated a new space. HH Architects was commissioned from the outset and worked with the church's leadership to research and acquire the heaven-sent, 138-acre site in Plano.

A tremendous undertaking to say the least, the HH professionals commenced with their tried and true "four 'd' master plan approach"—discover, define, design, deliver. In discovering where the church had been in terms of facilities and programs, they were able to define where it was going—five years and a few decades down the road—and then design architecture that would not only complement but also bolster the church's ability to achieve its goals. Once the well-thought-out plan had been devised, it was shared with the congregation in bigger-than-life, Texas style: A large presentation model and a three-dimensional, digital flythrough of the prospective place of worship was created and set to the score of "Majesty," a universal favorite, modern-day hymn, for added impact upon virtually entering the worship center.

Aesthetically, Prestonwood presents itself as a cutting-edge work of architecture that is equally welcoming to traditional churchgoers and those who attend on a more intermittent basis. The pastor sought a structure that looked like none other and had an appealing sporty draw to which the architects responded with a crisp palette of stone, brick—like that of Arlington's famed ballpark—and glass.

ABOVE LEFT: In a sculptural use of simple yet timeless elements, stone columns support the metal framing and stained glass.
Photograph by Craig D. Blackmon, FAIA

ABOVE RIGHT: Three distinct seating areas create an intimate feel despite the worship center's tremendous volume. Excellent lighting, acoustics and a state-of-the-art image magnification system and screen enhance the space for worship and praise.
Photograph by Craig D. Blackmon, FAIA

FACING PAGE: Recalling traditional elements, the large atrium gathering space has a vaulted ceiling and an interesting structural composition.
Photograph by Craig D. Blackmon, FAIA

A throwback to the European tradition of didactic art, an extensive series of stained glass depictions grace the façade's clerestory level—each book of the *Bible* is illustrated on its own panel.

Before worshippers even walk through the door, they are struck by the stunning architectural composition; and as they familiarize themselves with the seamless flow between a variety of spaces, they begin to realize the depth of Prestonwood's ministries. Known for its 1,000-member pageants and inspirational Sunday messages alike, the auditorium is the heart of the master-planned religious development. While it seats a staggering 7,200 people, the three-tier horseshoe arrangement, excellent audio-visual and acoustic technology and elegant lighting combine for an incredibly intimate setting. Evangelical churches are about community and connecting; the architecture that is Prestonwood connects people not only horizontally but also vertically with God. ■ ■ ■ ■ ■ ■ ■ ■ ■ ■ ■ ■

SMU Dedman Life Sciences Building

F&S Partners Incorporated

■ ■ ■ ■ ■ ■ ■ ■ ■ ■ ■ The dedication of Southern Methodist University's Dedman Life Sciences Building in 2001 was a momentous occasion in the history of one of Dallas' most prominent institutions of higher education. It provided a new future for SMU's natural sciences curriculum, elevating the university's teaching and research capabilities with first-class laboratories. The new building also allowed SMU to reallocate space in the adjacent Fondren Science Building, a landmark structure designed in the 1940s and renovated in 2003 with F&S Partners' help, further enhancing its programs in the other science disciplines. Associate Dean Randy Phillips relays his enthusiasm for the Dedman project: "It was a quantum leap for us ... to go from what we were in, which was an excellent building in 1948 but showing the wear of 50 years, to an efficient and comfortable building that supports outstanding teaching and cutting-edge research."

FACING PAGE: The Dedman Life Sciences Building uses the traditional Collegiate Georgian vocabulary of neighboring buildings to blend with the renowned campus architecture of SMU.
Project Design Team: G. Allen Atkinson Jr., Rick Jin, J. Steven Warrick, James C. Patton and Kenda Draper.
Photograph by Craig D. Blackmon, FAIA

The Dedman Life Sciences Building represents a highly successful collaborative effort between architect and client, established from a solid, longtime relationship. Both the architectural firm, F&S Partners Incorporated, a 45-year-old Dallas-based company that specializes in designing projects for universities, and the leadership of SMU felt strongly that this building should reflect the rich heritage and character of the SMU campus architecture. The campus is renowned for its traditional Collegiate Georgian style of architecture, exemplified from its first building, Dallas Hall, and a continuum of work by prominent Dallas architect Mark Lemmon, throughout the 1940s.

The careful allocation of resources, along with a collaborative project team, led by veteran architect and principal-in-charge Allen Atkinson, AIA, resulted in a new building that complements neighboring structures on the campus and reflects the timeless tradition of SMU. The design of the three-story, 68,100-square-foot brick and cast-concrete building places the offices and research laboratories for faculty and post-doctorial students in accordance with the sequence of windows, an invaluable perk for individuals who spend a vast majority of daylight hours indoors teaching and conducting research. The labs, which require complex air filtration systems and utilities, were consolidated in one vertical zone of the building. Flexibility and modularity were keys to designing new life sciences laboratory facilities, to allow the size and dimensions of laboratory spaces to change as the needs and people change. Today, the state-of-the-art facility has enabled SMU to attract top-notch researchers and teachers who conduct

highly sophisticated studies of infectious agents, diseases and aging, among others. With SMU's place in the scientific community

firmly established, the National Institutes of Health, National Science Foundation and American Heart Association have financially

backed the university's first-rate scientists and their studies. Indeed, the effects of the thoughtfully designed Dedman Life Sciences

Building will be felt well into the future, on an institutional, regional and global level. ▪ ▪ ▪ ▪ ▪ ▪ ▪ ▪ ▪ ▪ ▪ ▪

ABOVE LEFT: The undergraduate science teaching laboratories, such as this biology lab—designed using the modular lab planning approach—are adaptable for teaching different life science disciplines.
Photograph by Craig D. Blackmon, FAIA

ABOVE RIGHT: The lobby carries the Georgian style to the interior through details such as the wood wall paneling, decorative ceiling mouldings, entry columns and limestone flooring with granite accents.
Photograph by Craig D. Blackmon, FAIA

FACING PAGE: To achieve the Collegiate Georgian design, designers emphasized the architectural detailing, including the dominant windows and cast stone and masonry expression of the main entry.
Photograph by James Wilson

Yvonne A. Ewell Townview Center

Jennings*Hackler & Partners, Inc.

■■■■■■■■■■■ Prompted by a federal desegregation court order, the architect appeared before Judge Barefoot Sanders to declare: "I, Grady Jennings, do solemnly swear that Dallas' Townview Center will be one of the finest schools in the country."

The project began in 1984, but when funding for the consolidation of six specialty magnet schools fell through, construction was tabled. Plans sat dormant for more than a decade until Jennings*Hackler & Partners received word that the project was "a go." Only one problem ... the budget had been cut from a projected $40-$50 million to a more modest $30 million, to which the architects sanguinely responded with clever layout workarounds, a few less

FACING PAGE: The heavily trafficked Main Street corridor connects to academic core classrooms with an enclosed canopy of skylights taking advantage of the natural light from Dallas' frequent sunny days.
Project Design Team: Grady Jennings, Robert Hackler and Ken Jay.
Photograph by Michael Lyons

amenities and a slightly smaller yet equally impressive 340,000-square-foot campus. The long awaited dream was realized in 1997, as what is now known as the Yvonne A. Ewell Townview Center greeted more than 2,000 eager-to-explore students.

Overlooking the Trinity River and downtown business district, Townview Center possesses a professional, collegiate-like ambience that gives everyone from freshman to senior a taste of working world excitement and inspires students to stay focused on their career studies. Individual schools are connected by the light-infused Main Street corridor, which is an interesting space through which to travel and fulfills massive traffic flow needs. Consolidating the magnet schools in one location not only translates to efficient use of space, with a common library, computer center, multipurpose dining hall and wellness facility—where students are encouraged to sample lifelong sports such as racquetball, tennis, aerobics or jog on the outdoor track—but unites teenagers with peers who have different interests and aptitudes.

Townview Center was conceived to be a centralized magnet that would house six existing schools from various parts of the city under one roof: Talented and Gifted, Law and Government, Health Professions, Science and Engineering, Business and Management, Education and Social Services. The cross-pollination-like result enriches the educational experience.

TOP LEFT: A beautiful view along the east side of the building looking north toward downtown allows students to be inspired by the vibrant Dallas skyline in the distance.
Photograph by Michael Lyons

BOTTOM LEFT: The south building's spacious main entrance is centered along the sloping site and marked ceremoniously by the United States and Texas flags.
Photograph by Michael Lyons

FACING PAGE LEFT: Sleek, contemporary steel and glass railings surround the naturally skylit student stairways and approach to the entrance of Main Street.
Photograph by Michael Lyons

FACING PAGE RIGHT: An open perspective as seen from a sitting place within the welcoming 1,000-seat multipurpose/dining area is ready to accommodate the student body and faculty.
Photograph by Michael Lyons

The talented and gifted put their 400-seat theater to good use, while students in the Law and Government school enjoy their moot courtroom replete with jury box and judge's bench. Those with a knack for health professions, have the run of a mock hospital room, hospital kitchen and dental lab. Science and Engineering students are engaged in physics, chemistry, electronics and microscopy labs. A fully functional daycare interests students in the Education and Social Services school, and an actual functioning bank and travel agency setting is a delightful resource for business- and management-oriented teens.

Townview Center is a place like none other, and educators enjoy the facility as much as their students. Considered a state-of-the-art design in the mid-'90s, personal computer work stations for each teacher and multiple computer docks within each classroom are appreciated equally today and demonstrate

tremendous foresight on the architects' part. Though the entire architectural design team, including Grady Jennings, AIA, undoubtedly delighted in the unique opportunity, perhaps Bob Hackler, AIA, a high school teacher and college professor in his first career, enjoyed it most. ■ ■ ■ ■ ■ ■ ■ ■ ■ ■

CHAPTER FOUR
Industry Leaders

Gone are the days of stark white, sterile-feeling health care buildings and unimaginative institutional establishments. Amazing commercial complexes and research facilities showcase some of the most dazzling and innovative architecture to date.

First impressions are paramount, and architects are charged with creating the intangible "experience" before the actual experience even begins. Among these pages this magic is showcased in Urban Design Group's Gladney Center for Adoption; corporate projects such as the TGS Architects-designed EDS Credit Union and the Gensler-designed Baker Botts Dallas; and health care facilities including RTKL's The Heart Hospital Baylor Plano and Azimuth's Pine Creek Medical Center.

These industry projects are as expansive as they are costly, so the community is duly engaged, perhaps more so in these enterprises than in any other. The talented professionals who have created the featured buildings are very conscience of this fact; it is what drives them to exceed the high expectations set forth from inception.

Bank of America Plaza, Rees Associates, Inc. (formerly JPJ Architects, Inc.), page 168

RadioShack Riverfront Campus, HKS, Inc., page 208

Granite Park, BOKA Powell, page 154

Granite Park

■ ■

BOKA Powell

■ ■ ■ ■ ■ ■ ■ ■ ■ ■ ■ As developers become increasingly more inclined to incorporate a multitude of services and facilities with new business development, traditional office buildings are giving way to vibrant mixed-use developments in which office space is merely one component of the larger environment. Well-versed in designing and planning a wealth of commercial office developments around the globe, BOKA Powell's deft planning and implementation of the Granite Park mixed-use development embodies the future of multifunctional, enduring commercial office space.

Located in rapidly growing Plano, and originally conceptualized and built during the late '90s, phases I and II of Granite Park included a pair of class-A, 10-story office buildings that provided more than 525,000 square feet of prime office space, in addition to a five-level parking garage and 68,000 square feet

of retail. So well-received were these enduring structures that Granite Park Three, an iconic 14-story office structure with additional retail and parking facilities, was added to the site in 2006.

The three separate office buildings, which collectively comprise nearly 1 million square feet of premium workspace, provide employees with fantastic views thanks to floor-to-ceiling glass, as well as desirable on-site settings at which to lounge during breaks and leisure time. Granite Park One and Two front a pair of tranquil ponds, which are home to ducks and an ambient waterfall brook, and provide a serene backdrop to the rest of the inviting courtyard area. Sculpture, outdoor café seating and picnic space further adorn this welcoming social area, which is often used as a backdrop for weddings and family portraits.

Besides providing an enchanting outdoor space to Granite Park patrons, these aqueous elements serve the pertinent role of holding water for the park, so as not to overload storm drainage systems. Softscape and hardscape elements are gracefully interwoven around the ponds, fulfilling the needs for controlled drainage systems and functional pedestrian traffic zones in an aesthetically pleasing landscape. Moreover, terraces safely approach the water's edge, an uncommon element in suburban developments, further enhancing the site's interactivity with the water.

The office towers provide workers with first-class environments thanks to sophisticated public areas, covered parking, efficient elevators, ample and well-appointed restrooms, glass exteriors and efficient mechanical and building

ABOVE LEFT: The west elevation has a striking diagonal element.
Photograph courtesy of BOKA Powell

ABOVE RIGHT: A notch in the south elevation's massing separates building façade elements.
Photograph courtesy of BOKA Powell

FACING PAGE: The main lobby has decorative light fixtures and boasts art from Tim deJong and Jimmy Harwell.
Photograph courtesy of BOKA Powell

systems. The main lobbies exude an aura of elegance thanks to soft woods, elevated ceilings, back-painted glass, art from Tessie Nolan and decorative light fixtures and art from Tim deJong and Texas native Jimmy Harwell. Revolving entry doors combine with the 18-foot-high ceilings to convey interior movement outward. Efficient building systems include state-of-the-art cooling and condenser water loop systems, dual power sources for buildings and an effective air filtration system that exceeded building requirements, resulting in exceptional indoor air quality.

The towers themselves emphasize strength in simplicity. Grand in scale, the structures' glass exteriors emanate a modern style that is accented by a carefully planned slash across the façade that creates visual interest toward the entry. The tops of the buildings feature a subtle curvature that, when struck by light, creates a powerful visual dynamic. Movement is further fashioned in the form of a generous spire that features an LED light, which shines at night and is programmed for various colors during holidays.

Granite Park's impeccable office space is further enhanced by the enticing retail environments, banking facilities, waterside restaurants and on-site hotel facilities. All extensively planned around the centerpiece park and water features, these elements combine to provide Granite Park patrons with an engaging destination that offers a wide range of activities for both business and pleasure. Boldly planned and implemented by the skilled team at BOKA Powell, Granite Park represents the burgeoning future of mixed-use development, presciently planned years ago. ■ ■ ■ ■ ■ ■ ■ ■ ■ ■ ■ ■

ABOVE LEFT: Two serene ponds are home to ducks and a waterfall brook, providing a tranquil backdrop to the inviting courtyard area.
Photograph courtesy of BOKA Powell

ABOVE RIGHT: Aesthetics asides, these ponds serve the pertinent role of holding water for the site so as not to overload storm drainage systems.
Photograph courtesy of BOKA Powell

FACING PAGE: The elegant west lobby features high ceilings, soft woods and polished stone.
Photograph courtesy of BOKA Powell

AVW-TELAV

■ ■

Azimuth : Architecture, Inc.

■ ■ ■ ■ ■ ■ ■ ■ ■ ■   For a company in the business of devising creative audio-visual solutions, Azimuth Architecture employed contemporary

forms, a beautifully distilled material palette and expertise in the manipulation of light to create a commanding work of architecture within conservative

financial parameters and an aggressive design and construction schedule.

Among the first modern structures to be erected in Pinnacle Park—the site of an abandoned concrete-batching plant—AVW-TELAV's headquarters

had an almost immediate revitalizing effect on the area, which is now almost completely built out. Its hillside location and resultant vistas of downtown

ABOVE: Expert planning maximized the sloping site—a large, built-in retaining wall was incorporated into the design. The added clear height enabled the creation of a black box presentation space.
Rendering by Ryan Tharel, Azimuth : Architecture, Inc.

FACING PAGE: The two-story, 125,000-square-foot structure houses a variety of uses, and its open interior layout affords flexibility for the company's constantly evolving needs.
Project Design Team: John Taylor and Amy Shacklett.
Photograph by James F. Wilson

Dallas more than make up for the hurdles inherent to the land. Bordered by an escarpment that, for environmental protection purposes, could not be disturbed, the sloping site mandated clever drainage solutions and a built-in retaining wall. The architects used the property's topographic differential to their advantage by fastidiously devising the floor plan. With the corporate offices positioned above the showroom, the latter space gained greater floor-to-ceiling volume, giving AVW professionals a broader backdrop to formulate and test their production setups.

Second only to the fixed characteristics of the site, lighting proved vital to the architectural design. In contrast to the lobby's light, striking ambience with its abundance of natural light, medium-toned flooring and darkened ceiling, recessed entries were built into the tilt-wall façade to produce pockets of shade without inhibiting the views. AVW's projection systems were incorporated to create a dramatic, theatrical effect: The company's logo is projected onto a feature wall and free-floating planes with halogen lights create bright pools on the floor. In close proximity to the light-infused lobby, the architects created a "black box" environment for the media room, designed as a presentation space for AVW equipment installations.

Celebrating the materiality of substances—from the exterior's panes of glass, concrete walls and steel canopy entrance detail to the interior's steel stairway with cabling as rails—is a design aesthetic in its own right. At the top of the stairs, clients get a behind-the-scenes glimpse at the inner workings of AVW with an eagle's-eye view of team members pulling technologies to deliver or mocking up audio-visual plans in the distribution center. Multiple uses are housed in the two-story, 125,000-square-foot structure, and the open interior layout affords flexibility for the company's growing, changing needs. AVW's architecture eloquently demonstrates that which it offers its clients: a harmonious melding of design and technology. ■ ■ ■ ■ ■ ■ ■ ■ ■ ■

TOP RIGHT: The tone of AVW's lobby is immediately set through the combination of natural light, the darkened ceiling, the logo feature wall and free-floating planes.
Photograph by Charles Davis Smith, AIA

BOTTOM RIGHT: The building exterior celebrates its materials and construction with panes of glass, patterned concrete panels, a vertical intersecting wall and steel canopy entrance details.
Photograph by James F. Wilson

FACING PAGE: Visitors get a glimpse into the media room and distribution center from the top of the interior's contemporary steel stairway.
Photograph by Charles Davis Smith, AIA

Baker Botts Dallas

Gensler

■ ■ ■ ■ ■ ■ ■ ■ ■ ■ ■ Young companies often rely on the aesthetic of classical architecture swathed in dark wood paneling and decorated with pastoral artwork and generic items like painted-wood ducks and old books to demonstrate stability. But when an organization has been around as long as the state of Texas and maintained its position on the forefront of technology all along the way, its goals, prerogatives and creative options are strikingly different. On the underpinning of a three-decade-long, transatlantic working relationship, Gensler—an internationally acclaimed architecture firm that celebrated its 40th anniversary in 2005—and Baker Botts—a world-renowned law firm with roots back to 1840—blended their creative energies to renovate seven floors of prime law-office space overlooking Dallas' Arts District.

FACING PAGE: Timeless materials coupled with classic furnishings create the aperture for the modern glass art wall that reflects the Dallas Arts District skyline beyond the reception.
Project Design Team: Judy Pesek, Cindy Simpson, John Harrison and Scott McAllister.
Photograph by Nick Merrick, Hedrich Blessing Photography

Tasked with designing an office that at once supported Baker Botts' global brand and captured the unique flavor of its Texas heritage, the architects of Gensler commenced the design process with a careful assessment of how people interacted with the existing architecture and one another. They determined that consolidating meeting rooms and most of the common areas to one main floor would make better use of space and promote a greater sense of camaraderie between the various legal departments. Whereas the likelihood of a trial attorney and a real estate attorney running into one another, much less striking up any sort of conversation, was nil in the original space, the new layout ensured that a broad mixture of people were bound to mingle at any given moment.

Because first impressions can have such a profound impact, the Gensler team seized the opportunity to turn Baker Botts' 11th floor into not only the home of a state-of-the-art conference center but also a showpiece—one that welcomes staff members, instills confidence in clients and expresses to the community a genuine patronage of the arts. The sense of arrival is defined by a beautiful art wall that reflects passersby as well as pixels of the Dallas skyline. New York artist and Yale professor Sarah Oppenheimer championed the architects' vision with her expressive piece entitled *DPI*, a nod to the city as a hub of energy and technology—industries in which Baker Botts has long been involved—but on a

TOP LEFT: Precision is imperative to the modular design of this state-of-the-art conference center. Every plane is designed on a 2-foot by 2-foot grid to reinforce order and symmetry. The order is counterbalanced with the richness and warmth of diverse materials integrated throughout.
Photograph by Nick Merrick, Hedrich Blessing Photography

BOTTOM LEFT: Large panes of glass allow the conference room to be infused with natural light, connecting the outdoors with the interior spaces and creating a pleasant working environment.
Photograph by Nick Merrick, Hedrich Blessing Photography

deeper level echoes the precise nature of practicing law. While this piece is certainly a focal point, the architecture itself is a work of art, cleverly oriented to take in views of landmarks like the Nasher Sculpture Center, Dallas Museum of Art and Meyerson Symphony Center.

An art enthusiast by every definition, Baker Botts Dallas' principal-in-charge, Jack Kinzie, sought a chic setting to not only conduct business but also feature the firm's newly expanded collection of art. The architects of Gensler espoused his passion and created architecture with a contemporary yet timeless aesthetic, a comfortable yet highly professional ambience. ■ ■ ■ ■ ■ ■ ■ ■ ■ ■ ■ ■

ABOVE LEFT: Multipurpose rooms are a key trend in today's law firm world, providing an arena to gather, collaborate and relax while affording the flexibility of various venues.
Photograph by Nick Merrick, Hedrich Blessing Photography

ABOVE RIGHT: Breathtaking breccia royal stone in juxtaposition with the classic absolute-black marble wall creates an envelope of contemporary design that is cradled by the warmth of Jerusalem gold limestone flooring.
Photograph by Nick Merrick, Hedrich Blessing Photography

Bank of America Plaza

■ ■

Rees Associates, Inc. (formerly JPJ Architects, Inc.)

■ ■ ■ ■ ■ ■ ■ ■ ■ ■ The architects of JPJ Architects—now REES—were commissioned by Bramalea, a Canadian-based developer, to design a 2 million square-foot building that would appeal to full-floor tenants: companies demanding speedy elevator service, floor plans with usable space and excellent layout potential, more than just a handful of corner offices, unobstructed views and an aesthetically pleasing façade with landmark presence. The initial step toward meeting these objectives was devising a piggyback elevator system—the first project in the city to incorporate the technique—which significantly influenced the floor plate arrangement by reducing the elevator shaft requirements.

FACING PAGE: Just as the bank has undergone transitions in name and ownership over the years, so too has the firm that created it, keeping pace with the development of Dallas business. Bank of America Plaza's grand entry boasts a delightful interplay of geometric forms, reflectivity, translucency and light.
Project Design Team: Donald E. Jarvis, Bill Smith and Richard Flatt.
Photograph by Gregg Hursley

To ensure that the large floor plates would not make the building appear unattractively thickset, the architects devised plans for vertical loads on 16 large columns located 20 feet within the perimeter curtain wall; this creative structural solution allowed the building to be, at the time of its construction, the slenderest of its monumental height in the world. By offsetting the corners, floors average about 16 corner offices each and, sans distracting support columns, boasts panoramic views. The material palette further minimizes the building's footprint and enhances its visibility. Clear glass with a hint of light silver "celebrates the street by allowing the lobby to weave itself into the fabric of the city in a welcoming gesture to passersby," relates a REES architect. Bank of America Plaza's double-paned glass, with anodized aluminum mullions, sparkles brightly during the day and glows as it reflects the sunset.

The glass itself is energy efficient, yet the architects know that people are the greatest contributors to heat gain, so they utilized a proven cooling technique by creating a system whereby the building would generate cold water during off-peak hours and then pump the chilled liquid through air conditioning coils the next day for hours of inexpensive energy.

ABOVE LEFT: An artful architectural design and clever structural engineering allow more than a dozen corner offices on each level to have unobstructed views of the city.
Photograph by Gregg Hursley

ABOVE RIGHT: The brightly hued sculpture punctuates the powerful presence of the building, which is evident from every vantage—especially looking skyward from the base.
Photograph by Gregg Hursley

FACING PAGE: Erected in 1984, the 72-story building glimmers at night, with its signature, sculptural character eloquently expressed in the unique argon tube lighting.
Photograph by Gregg Hursley

Bank of America Plaza's design was orchestrated by the late Donald E. Jarvis, FAIA, a principal of JPJ, revered for his remarkable creativity, who alas did not see the project come to fruition—Bill Smith, FAIA, and Richard Flatt were also instrumental in its success. Thousands of people enjoy it daily, arriving at the adjacent double-helix parking structure, traveling through underground pedestrian passageways and rising to their destinations in elevators adorned with interchangeable, custom-woven tapestries that echo the structure's artful quality. The building has had a profound revitalizing effect on Dallas' historic West End and stands today as timeless as when it was conceived. ▪ ▪ ▪ ▪ ▪ ▪ ▪ ▪ ▪ ▪

Baylor Regional Medical Center at Plano

■ ■

PageSoutherlandPage

■ ■ ■ ■ ■ ■ ■ ■ ■ ■ Baylor Regional Medical Center at Plano is truly a groundbreaking campus for the Dallas-based Baylor Healthcare System. Being the first new green-field hospital campus in the Baylor Healthcare System in more than 30 years, Baylor wanted to take advantage of this opportunity and make the facility something special. Putting "hospitality back into the hospital," the medical center redefines hospital stereotypes by providing large rooms, comfortable beds, warm lighting and appetizing food. The center has been designed to blend two previously polarized concepts: vital medical care and warm hospitality. While in the caring hands of the hospital system, patients are treated to Baylor's luxury hotel-type environment. This begins immediately upon arrival. A guest may choose the valet service or the parking garage, which is directly adjacent to the medical office building and the main hospital facility. Minimizing all travel distances, the latter buildings themselves are connected by a sky bridge.

FACING PAGE: Tl e hospital and medical office building offer views to the beautifully landscaped health care campus.
Project Design Team: Mattia Flabiano III, W. Dee Maxey, Joshua Theodore, Britt Feik and E. Lynn Broyles.
Photograph by Craig D. Blackmon, FAIA

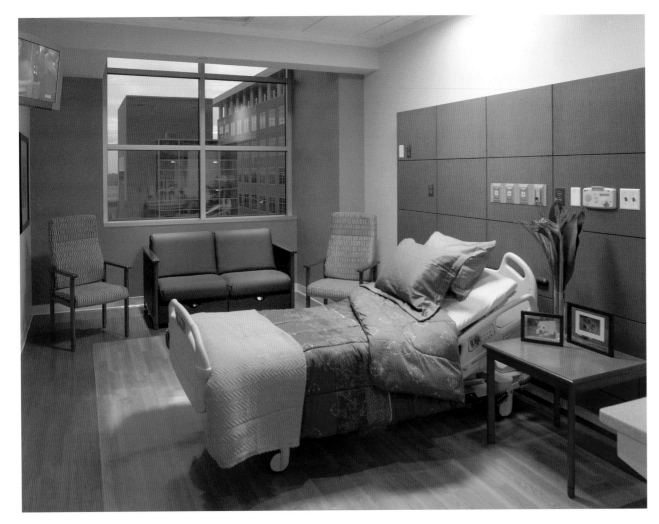

Inside, the colors are warm and a blend of natural light and stone can soothe any ailing person. Whenever possible a view to the outside world—including the Dallas skyline—has been utilized, allowing an open feel to corridors and the family lounge, and assisting guest orientation through points of reference. The guests' rooms are large, floored with wood-like sheet vinyl to meet aesthetic and sterility requirements and the beds have handcrafted headboards. While staying, guests have access to a variety of healthful, delicious foods on the room service menu, delivered by a staff member dressed in hotel-attendant attire. Easy access to the garden level and terraced courtyard remains constant to provide guests with the healthy benefits offered by the outdoors. High ceilings and large windows reiterate the impact of natural light, allowing a great deal of it to filter into the building.

Fully outfitted with state-of-the-art equipment, the seven-story health center boasts three floors of space dedicated to skilled medical attention. Ranging in size from 600 to 880 square feet, the 12 operating rooms feature voice-command response and direct video communication with Baylor's Dallas campus, keeping the hospital competitively up-to-date. Various quarters are attractively dedicated

ABOVE LEFT: Patient rooms are designed to provide a sense of warmth and hospitality to patients and family members alike.
Photograph by Craig D. Blackmon, FAIA

ABOVE RIGHT: Public areas have an inviting and hotel-like atmosphere, which was created with arriving patients and members of their family in mind.
Photograph by Craig D. Blackmon, FAIA

FACING PAGE LEFT: The medical office building and hospital are connected by tree-lined walkways in an urban pedestrian setting.
Photograph by Craig D. Blackmon, FAIA

FACING PAGE RIGHT: The medical center features a tiered healing garden with winding paths and outdoor seating.
Photograph by Craig D. Blackmon, FAIA

to an array of issues, ranging from physical therapy and general emergency services to highly specialized neurology, spine and orthopedic surgical care. The recovery wing happily removed traditional visitation restrictions, allowing families as much time together as they desire.

Designed by PageSoutherlandPage, Baylor Regional Medical Center at Plano had its fair share of challenges during design and construction. The firm had to convert what was originally intended as a heart hospital into a community-based specialty hospital, which required a major revamp, switching from

a heart diagnostic and treatment-centered facility to one with more holistic purposes. The firm, along with the Baylor Healthcare System, kept a strong focus on the interior to create something contemporary but warm and inviting—in a timeless modern style. ■ ■ ■ ■ ■ ■ ■ ■ ■ ■ ■

Bramhall Medical Office Building

William Peck & Associates, Inc.

■ ■ ■ ■ ■ ■ ■ ■ ■ ■ Bramhall Medical Office Building is a successful blend of historic design and modern functionality. Located within the Lewisville Old Town Design District, the medical building needed to meet strict historical design standards and blend into the turn-of-the-century surrounding. The building however, still needed to provide modern comfort and convenience while incorporating energy-efficient and sustainable design. Some of the energy efficient features include foam insulation, low-E wood windows, a variable-speed air handler and solar shading.

The nearly 10,000-square-foot building is situated in a district of renovated commercial and residential buildings from the late 1800s and houses two separate medical practices. Other new construction in the area—including several projects by William Peck & Associates—blends seamlessly with the historic district. The exterior of the Bramhall building is highly detailed deep red brick and buff-colored cast stone. Because it is set back from the street

FACING PAGE: The Bramhall building's deep red brick and buff-colored cast stone exterior reflects the surrounding historic district.
Photograph by Craig D. Blackmon, FAIA

and behind another building, it became important to give it a commanding presence. This was accomplished through its details, including the entry tower.

The nature of the project required historical research, involving detailed examination of regional and period photographs, plus interviews with residents. The interior continues the style and blends it with Art Deco and Old West elements. Reminiscent of a converted warehouse, pendant fluorescent lights are used along with galvanized metal countertops; playful Old West furnishings and artwork; and a reception desk framed by a standing seam metal roof.

Victorian, Craftsman and other traditional styles from the period dot the district. This gave the design team a creative template for the project. Reclaimed hard pine from a nearby home became the floor in the entrance of the doctor's practice, and windows, recovered from the home as well, line an interior hallway. Floor joists from the house were also salvaged and used as stair treads.

Many of the office's patients are children, so the Old West whimsy is reflected in an indoor playhouse styled after a cowboy-era jail and constructed from reclaimed material. The physician's wife, whose personal touch gives the entire design warmth and charm, skillfully decorated the interior. The blend of historic details and modern savvy is a successful one that has lead to similar projects in the area that combine late-1800s' style with modern sensibility. ■ ■ ■ ■ ■ ■ ■ ■ ■ ■ ■

LEFT: The reception area continues the exterior's theme with a standing-seam metal roof and period-inspired furnishings.
Photograph by Craig D. Blackmon, FAIA

FACING PAGE LEFT: The interior has a warm, Old West motif with environmentally friendly materials, such as the reclaimed wood floor.
Photograph by Craig D. Blackmon, FAIA

FACING PAGE RIGHT: The entry tower gives the Bramhall building a strong focal point while awnings over the windows provide energy-saving shade.
Photograph by Craig D. Blackmon, FAIA

The Container Store Headquarters

Rees Associates, Inc.

■ ■ ■ ■ ■ ■ ■ ■ ■ ■ When The Container Store's new corporate headquarters—store support facility—and distribution center went into operation, a team member rejoiced that he felt as though he had been given an emotional bonus because of the tremendous environment in which he was privileged to work. Nearly 1 million square feet all together, the wildly successful project was born of close collaboration between The Container Store's leadership and the professionals of REES, who assisted in developing the shell of the structures and designed all of the interior architecture, from the well-thought-out space plan to fixtures and finishes.

Richard J. Macri, vice president of REES and the project's design director, and his team set out to create not merely a functional space that would satisfy their client's needs but rather a space that would reflect the company's culture, anticipate its future needs and three-dimensionally define its style and

FACING PAGE: The central atrium's impressive volume, interesting geometric forms and vibrant colors combine for a pleasant, upbeat ambience.
Project Design Team: Richard J. Macri, Jan Blackmon, Michael Ufer, Frank Ragland, Jeannine Vail and Paul Ross.
Photograph by Craig. D. Blackmon, FAIA

mission. An intimate understanding of the corporate brand was achieved by spending time in the company's retail establishments, conducting benchmark research and asking the right questions to spur deeper thinking.

Enthusiasts of The Container Store enjoy the newness of each visit; even if the inventory offering has not significantly changed, something new seems to pop out every time. A similar visual interest was carried over to both the store support facility and distribution center—unlike many companies, whose offices are stunning and warehouses have economy-quality everything and are not particularly cheery. Workers in the 750,000-square-foot distribution center feel very much connected to their counterparts who spend their days strategizing at The Container Store's signature Elfa-brand workstations. Three pods house administrative offices, lockers and break rooms and the balance of space is devoted to rows upon rows of colorful shelving, accessed by tricycles and small-scale motorized vehicles.

The Mondrian-inspired palette of strong blue, red, black, white and yellow hues is appropriate because the modernist painter's creations echo the company's colors and philosophies on logic, containment and design; The Container Store's celebration of clean lines and beautiful, contemporary ideas is evidenced in its innovative line of products. Easily navigable, the L-shaped, two-story store support facility has legs of equal length that meet at a town center-like atrium. Main boulevards traverse both levels, leading to various department neighborhoods: product design, information technology support, logistics, marketing and merchandising, among others. Product references are subtly

LEFT: Clean, contemporary lines inform the distribution center's design.
Photograph by Craig. D. Blackmon, FAIA

woven throughout the space, from the abstracted barcode carpet pattern to iconic images like boxes and wrapping material, which are presented as both positive and negative space.

The home organization giant's fiscal responsibility inspired the architects to devise creative applications for somewhat ordinary, reasonably priced yet durable items, such as fluorescent lighting fixtures suspended in interesting patterns to illuminate the atrium and boulevards and create a sense of movement. On the underpinning of this exceptional project and the organizations' strong relationship,

The Container Store promptly commissioned REES to implement similar design elements of the store support facility in its retail locations as well as to design new stores, including several flagships, from Manhattan to Los Angeles. ■ ■ ■ ■ ■ ■ ■ ■ ■ ■

ABOVE LEFT: A few of The Container Store's innovative products are displayed as art in the main boulevard circulation corridor.
Photograph by Craig. D. Blackmon, FAIA

ABOVE RIGHT: The play of natural and artificial light creates interest in the central atrium.
Photograph by Craig. D. Blackmon, FAIA

EDS Credit Union

■ ■

TGS Architects

■ ■ ■ ■ ■ ■ ■ ■ ■ ■ When the credit union for EDS, a leading global technology services company, decided to relocate from the main EDS campus to a new corporate headquarters building as part of an expansion program, it only made sense that TGS Architects, having designed approximately 40 similar financial institution buildings, represented the consummate firm to handle such an undertaking. Realizing that the vast majority of the credit union members were EDS employees, who generally tend to be rather technologically savvy individuals, TGS designed a state-of-the-art credit union appropriately housed within a sublime contemporary structure.

FACING PAGE: The elegant front entry of the EDS Credit Union is gracious for its warm red brick and subtle white accents, which contrasts sharply with the striking, blue-tinted glass atrium.
Project Design Team: Dallas Taylor, Bill Ward, John Pizzarello and Amy Renno.
Photograph by Dallas Taylor

Early on in the project, TGS conducted a feasibility study and ascertained that it would actually be cheaper for the EDS Credit Union to build its own separate structure than to continue paying rent to office on the main EDS campus. After selecting a highly desirable corner location only blocks away from the campus, TGS proceeded to formulate a comprehensive project budget along with a bold contemporary design.

Utilizing split-faced masonry and warm red brick with white accents along much of the exterior base, the foundation of the building is subtle yet stately, which contrasts well with the striking blue-tinted glass—EDS' primary color—comprising the top of the edifice. The high-performance, low-E glass maximizes interior light while deflecting heat. A sophisticated lighting system makes the glass atrium glow at night, as finely tuned lights focus on polished, stainless steel discs about 15 to 20 feet up in the ceiling, which spray the light and effectively fill up the space.

The services afforded within this striking structure are fitting of its technologically proficient credit union members—for starters, the branch is completely automated; no tellers are needed. In the lobby, remote teller kiosks afford patrons efficient, highly functional stations, eliminating the wait typically associated with facilitating transactions at financial institutions. For patrons desiring to access their personal safe deposit box—a task historically characterized by being waited on by a bank employee, a series of signatures and the transfer of vault keys—the process has been streamlined thanks to the incorporation of biometrics, which use a thumbprint to confirm identity, followed by a simple password.

ABOVE LEFT: A sophisticated lighting system allows the atrium to glow at night, as stainless steel discs disperse light fully throughout the space.
Photograph by Mark Olsen

ABOVE RIGHT: Albeit this technologically advanced credit union is largely automated, a concierge desk affords genuine customer service.
Photograph by Mark Olsen

FACING PAGE: High-performance, low-E glass maximizes interior light while deflecting heat.
Photograph by Dallas Taylor

Wireless networking and computer stations in the lobby afford patrons a veritable internet café, while vibrating alert mechanisms—like the ones used by restaurants to signify a table is ready—notify members when their desired service is ready. Moreover, drive-thru banking features two-way audio and video interaction with tellers, further engendering the credit union's desired technologically advanced ambience.

Deftly designed by TGS Architects, the EDS Credit Union headquarters is a boldly contemporary structure, fitting of the functional and efficient services available within and a perfect fit for the progressive personnel comprising the credit union's membership. ■ ■ ■ ■ ■ ■ ■ ■ ■ ■ ■

Ericsson Village

MESA

■ ■ ■ ■ ■ ■ ■ ■ ■ ■ MESA's innovative ideas and environmental sensitivity added tremendous value to Ericsson Village because rather than recreating the site to behave in a particular manner, the landscape architects worked with the land to design an alluring corporate campus. Entrances were thoughtfully conceived to welcome employees and guests; buildings and paths were designed to complement the lake and meandering creek; the drainage swale was rerouted through the parking lot in a naturalistic, arcing pattern so that it could serve as both a functional and a design element; the parking lot was organized in a non-intrusive, circular pattern; and the hardscaping and landscaping were carefully designed to tastefully emphasize the site's inherent beauty and native plant life.

FACING PAGE: Whether people want to relax in solitude or at the water's edge among colleagues, the lakeside area boasts a variety of settings.
Project Design Team: Tary Arterburn and Chip Impastato.
Photograph by Charles Smith

Had the site been traditionally developed, the sloping land with significant grade changes would have been hastily leveled; MESA embraced the inherent challenges. The entry sequences—a formal entrance for welcoming dignitaries and other guests at the center and two employee entrances on either side of the campus—are primary points of interest. First welcomed by the large circle of annual plantings and then by the open, naturally landscaped site plan, people smoothly transition from the entrance into the buildings. Pedestrian paths are clear, easily navigable, and as people ceremonially make their way across the bridge scenic views unfold all around, even from garden spaces below. Though unobvious, the parking lot is at a second-floor elevation, which advantageously minimizes its presence—each row of parking boasts significant landscape screening, furthering this effect.

For sustainability as well as visual impact, Ericsson Village is graced predominantly by native plant materials, which require less maintenance, a smaller amount of water and tend to last much longer than their non-indigenous counterparts. The buffalo grass is mowed quarterly and the elms, burr oaks, eastern red cedars, soft-leaf yucca, inland sea oats and love grass hold their own in Texas' dynamic climate. The professionals of MESA consider the material palette to be fairly simple, yet the textural juxtaposition of these types of vegetation with each other and against the Granbury limestone retaining walls is breathtaking. The hardscape materials borrow from the natural color and texture of the site, creating cohesiveness between the built and natural environments.

LEFT: To reach the heart of the campus, employees and guests ceremonially pass over the main bridge, beneath which lie lushly landscaped gardens.
Photograph by Charles Smith

FACING PAGE LEFT: Beautiful and functional, the company's North American headquarters at Legacy Park features campus-wide wireless access, affording associates the flexibility to work at their desks or on their laptops by the water, mature-growth trees and verdant clearings.
Photograph by Charles Smith

FACING PAGE RIGHT: The intimate patios on the lakeside are ideal for gathering or working.
Photograph by Charles Smith

The lake and its myriad gathering spaces—from open plazas to intimate patios—are situated at the site's lowest level for enjoyment from vantage points of varying levels, inside and out. The area's design brings people right to the edge of the water and functions as an outdoor room for company-wide events. In juxtaposition, opposite the lake's hardscaped side, the water meets the vegetation in a nature-inspired, curvilinear manner. Though the lakeside area is vast and mass amounts of people can move about, it maintains an intimate feel.

The master planning of Ericsson Village's 100-acre site has garnered prestigious recognition from the American Society of Landscape Architects' Texas chapter, but the greater upshot is the projected long-term effects that the premier campus will have on the corporation's ability to recruit and retain top-notch employees. ▪ ▪ ▪ ▪ ▪ ▪ ▪ ▪ ▪ ▪ ▪

Gladney Center for Adoption

■ ■

Urban Design Group, Inc.

■ ■ ■ ■ ■ ■ ■ ■ ■ ■ ■ "Adoption has gone on since time began, from Moses to Angelina Jolie," relates Mike McMahon, the president of Gladney Center for Adoption, a Fort Worth-based organization with roots back to 1887. The center has always kept pace with the times, so when changing needs mandated a new facility, its leadership looked to The Amend Group—formerly WorkPlace USA—and Urban Design Group to translate its longstanding mission and vision for the future into a beautiful, welcoming, multifunctional space that would tell Gladney's story and the stories of those whose lives have been forever changed by it.

The managing principal of Urban Design Group's Dallas office, Ron Armstrong, was as excited about the project as the client. He appreciates that while an architect can spend his entire career signing his name to impressive projects, only if he is truly blessed does a project come along that trumps all others—

FACING PAGE: Nestled into a hillside, the new facility was built with private funds that were raised during an extended capital campaign.
Photograph by Steven Vaughan Photography, Dallas, 2007

not for its extravagant size or budget but for the uniqueness of the opportunity and the final result's broad-reaching, lasting significance. Led by The Amend Group, the architectural team began by working with Gladney to define goals and develop a master plan of the campus's uses. Only after the functional aspects of the project were organized did the team turn its attention to the aesthetics.

Complex relationships between the wide variety of people who interact with the center meant complexity of spaces within the building itself, so setting a universally appealing tone was paramount. The nonrestrictive fenestration and charming porte cochere establish an immediate sense of welcome, as do the subtle Texas theme and palette of organic materials—stone, wood, metal and glass. First-time visitors, children and adults alike are completely taken aback by the warm, inviting atmosphere—sans any notion of the grandiose. From the moment they walk through the door, they are acutely aware that Gladney is far more than an adoption center.

The center boasts a clever layout in which frequented areas—like the gallery and seminar rooms for community-outreach and pre- and post-adoption parenting programs—are located nearest the main entrance while the expectant young ladies' dormitory is at the far end of a private wing. Accommodating up to 30 mothers-to-be, the well-appointed residential area features a group dining room, crafts area, living room replete with fireplace and a pavilion. It is a safe place where people can open up and make tough decisions.

The professionals of Urban Design Group feel that architecture should create a sense of community, a sense of purpose, as well as define the collective personality of the people who interact with it. Their eloquent interpretation of Gladney's ideas resulted in a haven where a noble cause can progress. In the center's first 120 years, nearly 30,000 children were placed in "forever homes." ■ ■ ■ ■ ■ ■ ■ ■ ■ ■

The Heart Hospital Baylor Plano

■ ■

RTKL Associates, Inc.

■ ■ ■ ■ ■ ■ ■ ■ ■ ■ Who would have thought that inspiration for the exterior of a state-of-the-art healthcare facility would strike at sunset as an architect gazed through an airplane window? When RTKL Vice President John Castorina relayed his experience of noticing beacons of light—glimmering ponds—interspersed across the landscape to the hospital board and founding physicians, they were intrigued. John knew that he and his team could recreate the brilliant effect, architecturally, so that as passersby caught a glimpse of the tightly sited limestone building accented by large panels of dark glass embedded with silver strips, they would immediately recognize it as The Heart Hospital Baylor Plano.

FACING PAGE: The sculptural exterior of The Heart Hospital Baylor Plano is an outward indication of the upscale comfort, high-quality care and sophisticated technologies within.
Project Design Team: John Castorina, Keith Guidry, Jay Frisco, Eric Dinges, Stan Parnell, Shelley Jones and Aimee Platt.
Photograph by Charles Davis Smith

Determined to break the "hospital as sterile box" mold, the experts of RTKL applied their extensive heart hospital experience to this project. They analyzed the traffic flow of everyone who would work and stay at the hospital as well as the ease of navigability for visitors. Because they knew that each department would have different priorities and perspectives regarding the layout, the architects began brainstorming sessions with a number of separate small groups. They blended two groups to a happy compromise and added another and another until the room was full of people who were excited about the same plan.

Patients are referred to as guests and are treated as such in the five-star hotel-like hospital, which is replete with valet parking, concierge services, bedside check-in and gourmet meals served on fine china by a tuxedoed wait staff. The architecture that envelops this unique experience is what truly sets the stage for a healing stay—spaces are smartly organized so that appropriate staff, supplies and equipment are concentrated near the patient.

The building's unique bowtie shape—in addition to maximizing square footage—affords nurses direct lines of sight through the extra-wide doors into guests' private suites, all 68 of which boast artwork, a flat-screen television, internet access and expansive views to the outside. Because heart-related issues mandate more monitoring equipment than most other health concerns, the suites are

LEFT: The physician library, located on the penthouse level, provides a comfortable space for respite with internet access, lockers and expansive views to the outside. Photograph by Charles Davis Smith

FACING PAGE TOP: Glass curtain walls in public areas enhance wayfinding and make the coordination of exterior and interior materials especially evident. Photograph by Charles Davis Smith

FACING PAGE BOTTOM: Comfortably appointed patient rooms allow ample space for caregivers, visitors and the large array of medical equipment required for cardiovascular patients. Photograph by Charles Davis Smith

strategically laid out so that nothing, including people, needs to be shuffled around when doctors and nurses examine patients.

Brilliant yet long overdue, the double-corridor design elevates the hospital into a league of its own. Postoperative guests are expected to be up and about within one day of having surgery, and at The Heart Hospital Baylor Plano they can do it safely, as part of the hallway, just outside their rooms, is physically reserved for those moving slower than the staff's bustling pace. How one feels, both physically and emotionally, is indicative of how quickly one heals, and the curvilinear quality of the hospital not only makes recuperative walks seem shorter but evokes feelings of optimism as new, well-appointed vistas await just around each bend. ▪ ▪ ▪ ▪ ▪ ▪ ▪ ▪ ▪ ▪ ▪

NEC

■ ■

BOKA Powell

■ ■ ■ ■ ■ ■ ■ ■ ■ ■ Needing a new corporate campus that would integrate several diverse business units, global technology leader NEC engaged BOKA Powell to conduct an area-wide land search to locate a considerable expanse of terrain on which it could swiftly relocate and grow into over time. The team at BOKA Powell helped select an undeveloped, 28-acre tract in Las Colinas, which provided NEC with close proximity to the airport—a key provision of its desired locale—in one of Dallas' more high-profile corporate addresses.

Soon after, what began simply as a site search for BOKA Powell turned into a full-scale master plan. Intrigued by the location but not entirely convinced, NEC contacted BOKA Powell on a Friday, asking for an illustration of what a development on the proposed site would look like, and the design team deftly crafted a sketch over the weekend that exhibited how the main 10-story building addressed the corner at the intersection of Highways 161 and 114.

FACING PAGE: The main 10-story tower of NEC's corporate campus in Las Colinas creatively uses materials and building systems to clarify programmed elements, resulting in a timeless design.
Photograph by John W. Davis

The drawing was so cogent that NEC settled on that particular location, engaging BOKA Powell to perform full architectural design services.

First programming and master-planning the million-plus-square-foot campus, BOKA Powell then designed the two campus buildings' core and shell, eventually performing interior design duties as well. Designing facilities that are adaptable to future uses and tenants has long been a hallmark of BOKA Powell's designs, and that prescient thinking was exceptionally beneficial with this project. Over the past five-plus years, NEC's need for facilities decreased by approximately 200,000 square feet, but thanks to the flexible design, NEC has been able to keep its operations intact while leasing excess space to subtenants.

The main 10-story structure instantly catches the eye of passersby, thanks to an ingenious exterior lantern concept of stacked conference spaces. Lighting the building from the outside was a requirement of the Las Colinas Association, but this obligation was met in an innovative way by internally illuminating a lantern on each tower, which became the buildings' defining architectural element against the night skyline. Moreover, the two lanterns are linked via a brightly lit, connecting canopy that ties those elements together and accents the floor-to-floor glass exterior.

TOP LEFT: NEC's main lobby is gracious and inviting. BOKA Powell undertook all shell and interior design duties, in addition to programming and master planning the entire campus.
Photograph by John W. Davis

BOTTOM LEFT: The restaurant-style corporate dining center has durable yet elegant stained concrete floors.
Photograph by John W. Davis

FACING PAGE LEFT: The corporate tower and adjacent five-story R&D building are linked by their architectural fenestration, a colonnade and an innovative lantern lighting system devised by Don Powell.
Photograph by John W. Davis

FACING PAGE RIGHT: The building's floor-to-ceiling glass construction lacks spandrels, allowing for illuminated towers that define the building on the night skyline.
Photograph by BOKA Powell

The main building sits next to a five-story, L-shaped building that houses the research and development functions and is replete with high-tech equipment. Additional features of the NEC campus include an executive conference center intended for product demonstration and sales, which includes raised-floor areas allowing for plug-and-play capabilities, a full-service dining center with striking stained concrete floors and an immaculate fitness center—including men's and women's shower and locker rooms, exercise equipment and a weight room—on par with any local health club. ▪ ▪ ▪ ▪ ▪ ▪ ▪ ▪ ▪ ▪ ▪

Pine Creek Medical Center

Azimuth : Architecture, Inc.

■ ■ ■ ■ ■ ■ ■ ■ ■ ■ ■ Aside from the façade's healthcare-descriptive signage, someone lingering in Pine Creek Medical Center's light-infused entry rotunda could easily forget the reason for his or her visit, even mistake the aesthetically appealing space for a spa. Clean architectural lines, a well-organized layout, simple yet thoughtfully conceived detailing and a crisp palette of both organic and manmade materials—from stacked stone and richly stained wood paneling to large sheets of glass and brushed aluminum accents—combine to welcome guests and immediately set their minds at ease.

ABOVE: Pine Creek Medical Center's master plan brings to life the clients' goals of a modern, progressive facility with efficient patient flow and ease of expansion.
Rendering by Ryan Tharel / Azimuth : Architecture, Inc.

FACING PAGE: Building design elements include stone and brick exterior accents, copper facia and roofing, stone columns and accent wall natural redwood soffits and landscaped grounds and courtyard.
Project Design Team: Jack Atkins, Mary Bledsoe, Amy Shacklett and Jeff Cain.
Photograph by James F. Wilson

A healthful, rejuvenating, stylized lodge ambience is precisely what the clients had in mind, and through their active engagement with Azimuth Architecture, the project came to fruition on time, within the financial plan and much to the delight of the creative team as well as those who interact with it—doctors, nurses and patients, alike. The 2005-completed hospital proved so successful, in fact, that Azimuth was immediately commissioned to complete the balance of structures specified in the original master plan, which makes superb use of the site.

While all elements of Pine Creek Medical Center needed to function properly, perhaps the most critical aspect of the design was controlling public and private areas. The architects began by systematically developing the schematics through bubble diagram exercises—blocks of the program were transposed into units of space that when added together represent the layout of the state-of-the-art 46,000-square-foot facility. Imaging modalities were specified near the surgical area; human resources offices were positioned nearest the entry for patient and family consultations.

Among other features, the facility boasts nearly two dozen patient suites, a pharmacy, a café, an emergency suite, diagnostic imaging and rehabilitation departments as well as integrated operating room systems: the latest and greatest in computed tomography scanning, magnetic resonance imaging, wireless telemetry and digital imaging storage and retrieval systems. Azimuth's impressive repertoire of comparably complex projects provided a solid underpinning for its team to create a work of architecture that entices medical professionals in the upper echelon of their trade.

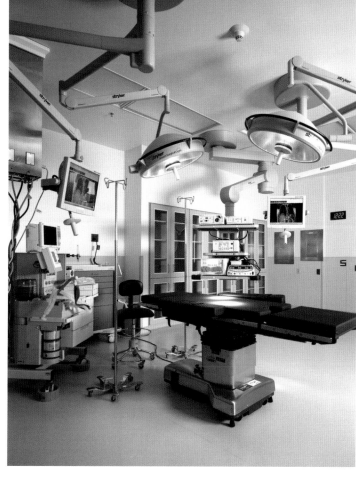

From the outset of the project, Azimuth's interior design team was actively engaged, offering creative solutions for space planning, as well as finish, artwork, furniture and accessories specification.

The warm interior design palette sets the tone for patients' experiences. From the comfortable leather seating, wood-veneered walls, stone fireplace and art niches of the entry rotunda to the built-in wardrobes, vanity areas and day beds in the private patient rooms, patients and visitors are treated to a new type of hospital environment—a soothing, restful, healing atmosphere. As a result of such close collaboration between architects, designers and the client, a consistent modern aesthetic weaves throughout the Pine Creek Medical Center, from the structure's innermost parts to its beautifully landscaped grounds. ■ ■ ■ ■ ■ ■ ■ ■ ■ ■ ■

ABOVE LEFT: The entry rotunda, including waiting area, serves as the focal point and core of the hospital, giving visitors a clear sense of arrival.
Photograph by James F. Wilson

ABOVE RIGHT: The four technologically advanced surgical suites incorporate ergonomic furniture, ceiling-mounted booms and consoles and the latest surgical tools used for video-assisted surgical procedures.
Photograph by Charles Kendrick & Co. Photography

FACING PAGE TOP: Comfortable leather seating, wood-veneered walls, stone fireplace and art niches with black & white photography further illustrate the "modern lodge" concept.
Photograph by Charles Kendrick & Co. Photography

FACING PAGE BOTTOM: Café on Pine Creek offers a relaxed setting for families and staff with views out to the landscaped courtyard, as well as outdoor dining.
Photograph by Charles Kendrick & Co. Photography

RadioShack Riverfront Campus

■ ■

HKS, Inc.

■ ■ ■ ■ ■ ■ ■ ■ ■ ■ Needing a modern facility to provide its 2,600 employees with a flexible, horizontally integrated workplace that encouraged efficiency and collaboration, RadioShack Corporation commissioned the national architecture/engineering firm HKS to plan, design and oversee construction of a seven-building, 900,000-square-foot campus at a confluence of two forks along the Trinity River.

An adaptive reuse project, the site previously had been home to subsidized housing that had fallen into disrepair—the tenants of which were assisted by RadioShack and the city in finding better, more affordable homes. Maintaining a valuable commitment to develop in the city of Fort Worth's downtown area, the construction of RadioShack's headquarters on the 37-acre, riverfront site reinforced the viability of downtown Fort Worth for future development—serving as an impeccable model of mutually satisfying collaboration between private industry and municipal government.

FACING PAGE: The modern, north façade of RadioShack's 900,000-square-foot campus is composed primarily of glass and shines brilliantly at night along the Trinity River.
Project Design Team: Dan Jeakins, Owen McCrory, David Meyer, Glenn Clarke and Jason Crist.
Photograph by Blake Marvin/HKS, Inc.

HKS, led by Dan Jeakins, AIA, and David Meyer, CID, took an extensive tour around the nation in search of similar urban campuses, finding very few. Locating a 35-plus-acre urban setting that fronted a river was a challenge, but Fort Worth ended up being a premier location. With the site adjacent to downtown Fort Worth, RadioShack wanted to be respectful of the city's architectural vernacular while at the same time creating a modern building. The result is a campus with essentially two faces: a south face that is considerate of downtown Fort Worth's brick vernacular and a modern exterior composed primarily of glass that faces the north.

Prior to the spring of 2005 when RadioShack began moving employees into this new facility, it had officed in a 1970s' era building that was vertically oriented, predicated on an old-workplace culture replete with private offices and few communal work areas. Thus, HKS designed a main street, which is connected to the 2,400-car parking garage and is utilized by all employees, that runs through the campus area with connectivity to all outlying buildings. The street is lined with stores offering employees various personal services and culminates with food service and a Starbucks. Moreover, the site itself featured a nearly 100-foot fall from the street to the river, which was downplayed through careful planning and the incorporation of an escalator along the main street.

Other communal elements of the all-wireless campus include a tiered amphitheater with adjoining meeting rooms, a 500-seat dining facility, which doubles as a group meeting area and has a cantilevered balcony overlooking the river, a fitness center and direct broadcast studios.

In addition to being highly functional and flexible, the campus effectively incorporated myriad Green building design elements and is LEED Silver certified. Energy-efficient materials, water conservation, an innovative under-floor air distribution system and a carefully crafted building envelope were a few of the elements that helped achieve this laudable distinction. ▪ ▪ ▪ ▪ ▪ ▪ ▪ ▪ ▪ ▪ ▪

ABOVE LEFT: A vast, double-height space makes a dramatic impact upon entering the RadioShack lobby. Photograph by Blake Marvin/HKS, Inc.

ABOVE RIGHT: The flagship StoreOne is a vibrant showcase of RadioShack's current and future technologies. Photograph by Blake Marvin/HKS, Inc.

FACING PAGE: Open, collaborative work areas encourage face-to-face interaction between employees. Photograph by Blake Marvin/HKS, Inc.

Southwest Airlines Federal Credit Union

TGS Architects

■ ■ ■ ■ ■ ■ ■ ■ ■ ■ ■ Southwest Airlines is well known for being an innovative, exceptionally unique brand characterized largely by its friendliness, warm colors and fun environment. So when the low-fare industry giant required a new credit union headquarters, it only made sense that TGS Architects develop a unique design solution, via a renovation of existing facilities plus several significant additions, apposite of Southwest Airlines' distinct corporate identity.

Examining the site's existing facilities, the project team at TGS Architects deduced that the new structures would combine with extant buildings to form an L-shape, and created an exciting arrival spot and prominent central atrium lobby by fashioning a bold pyramid structure at this intersection point. A captivating architectural form, the pyramid addresses the corner and provides a pronounced front entry through which patrons enter the credit union's

FACING PAGE: The ultra-modern design implemented at the Southwest Airlines Federal Credit Union is a highly functional sculpture that happens to double as a credit union.
Project Design Team: Dallas Taylor, Hiroshi Watanake, Bill Ward and John Pizzarello.
Photograph by Dallas Taylor

two-story central lobby area, in addition to separating the credit union from its adjacent neighbors. Once inside, credit union members are greeted by an exciting space replete with bright colors, predominately blues and purples, apropos of Southwest Airlines' lighthearted philosophy.

The pyramid is composed of a tubular steel frame system and translucent Skywall panels—high-performance sandwich panels utilizing special fiberglass insulation that allows light to pass through while deflecting heat—allowing natural light to filter through the skin into the main lobby. Brilliant in its own right, the pyramid is further accented by a sophisticated automated lighting system that emphasizes the skin's undulating shapes and colors, making its geometric form effectively glow in the evening.

The credit union's drive-thru facility is comprised of curved metal and shaped like an airplane wing, complementing the credit union's marketing program. The architecturally designed lighting system bathes the canopy of the drive-thru facility in light, highlighting this exceptional feature while providing a pertinent security function. TGS Architects also designed a two-story executive and operations space as

an extension of the pyramid, and provided site analysis, interior design, master planning and engineering services on the project as well.

An ultra-contemporary design appropriate for Southwest Airlines' progressive corporate identity, TGS Architects' renovation and expansion of the Southwest Airlines Federal Credit Union provided a strong architectural solution in the form of an exceptional, one-of-a-kind sculpture—albeit a highly functional sculpture. ■ ■ ■ ■ ■ ■ ■ ■ ■ ■ ■

ABOVE LEFT: The customer lobby, characterized by its playful, warm colors and engaging, oversized shapes, is reflective of Southwest Airlines' effervescent branding and corporate philosophy.
Photograph by Mark Olsen

ABOVE RIGHT: The two-story, central lobby area has a lighthearted and whimsical ambience thanks to the abundant natural light and ubiquitous purples, greens and blues.
Photograph by Mark Olsen

FACING PAGE: The pyramid shape is comprised of a tubular steel frame system and translucent Skywall panels, which allow natural light to filter in through the skin into the main lobby.
Photograph by Mark Olsen

Tenet Healthcare

■ ■

BOKA Powell

■ ■ ■ ■ ■ ■ ■ ■ ■ ■ When Tenet Healthcare required new office space for its headquarters, it envisioned the novel approach of developing adjacent office towers that allowed Tenet to lease the second tower to allied vendors, which provided the economic engine for its construction while fomenting an even grander perceived presence for Tenet.

Deftly designed by BOKA Powell, the 750,000-square-foot development's primary tower is a 16-story, build-to-suit structure that connects to the adjoining 13-story multitenant office tower via a highly functional yet aesthetically pleasing concourse level. Abutting a lunch café utilized by tenants of both towers, this visually engaging thoroughfare features full-height glass and also connects to the adjacent parking garage.

FACING PAGE: Tenet Healthcare's corporate campus provided a 16-story tower for the industry giant, as well as an adjacent 13-story tower that is utilized by Tenet's allied vendors. Photograph by Charles Davis Smith, AIA

Patrons to either tower are welcomed by immaculate, two-story lobbies that feature anigre wood, granite, French limestone and fluted zinc columns, all executed impeccably in terms of alignment, joinery and finishes. One thing BOKA Powell takes great pride in is blending interior and exterior building elements, and by effectively incorporating outside paving materials and other external aspects within, established a dually cohesive architectural environment. The building is often recognized for its trademark backlit cracked-glass accent panels that adorn the lobby and elevators.

Another pertinent principle of BOKA Powell's design philosophy is to create iconic, memorable buildings. Both edifices are outfitted with large-scale barrel vaults, which effectively cap the building and, along with the larger building's Tenet signage, create a dynamic presence against the sky. These transitional structures resemble traditional office buildings by virtue of their defined base, body and cap; albeit those

elements are fenestrated in a very modern fashion, featuring a subtle, salmon-colored skin that takes its cues from the nearby Galleria mall.

So successful were the design and execution on these office towers that BOKA Powell itself was a tenant for five years within the campus. Dually enjoying the development's first-rate facilities while benefiting from having an on-site example to showcase the firm's illustrious work, the creation of Tenet's headquarters campus was a mutually satisfying project for Tenet Healthcare and BOKA Powell. ■ ■ ■ ■ ■ ■ ■ ■ ■ ■

ABOVE LEFT: The double-height main lobby is comprised of refined elements such as granite, anigre wood, French limestone and cracked-glass accent panels.
Photograph by Charles Davis Smith, AIA

ABOVE RIGHT: Both towers are capped with impressive barrel vaults, which house necessary building systems while establishing a dynamic presence against the sky.
Photograph by Charles Davis Smith, AIA

FACING PAGE: A gracious, two-story front entry welcomes patrons inside, where exterior elements are carried in, establishing a cohesive architectural environment inside and out.
Photograph by Charles Davis Smith, AIA

The Webb @ LBJ

Edwin Brantley Smith & Associates, Inc.

■ ■ ■ ■ ■ ■ ■ ■ ■ ■ Those not familiar with Edwin Brantley Smith's work would likely have a difficult time imagining what is now The Webb @ LBJ—an aesthetically exquisite, refined structure that houses some of the nation's foremost companies—as a well-worn, windowless, vacant 350,000-square-foot mall with one tree on the entire expanse of property. Yet that is precisely the mixed media canvas Edwin was given. An artist as well as an architect, he saw beyond the modest façade and helped the developer envision a state-of-the-art structure with Texas-sized appeal that could be radically renovated within fairly modest monetary parameters and then leased in large units to long-term tenants, a far cry from the originally proposed Class-C office space.

FACING PAGE: Concrete pylons provide visual reinforcement for the entries of this high technology office complex. The facility is the adaptive reuse of a 42-year-old regional shopping center.
Photograph by Steven Vaughan Photography

The challenges were abundant, but Edwin and his team responded to each as an opportunity to be even more creative. Inescapably visible from the adjacent freeway overpasses, the building's one-story roof, which was unrestrainedly garnished with myriad antennas, rooftop units and other unsightly elements, emerged as a selling point. These elements were removed and new devices were rearranged and masked by a chic yet simple palette of materials.

An interesting repetition of large cylindrical forms veneered with custom composite aluminum panels gave new life to the roofline, balanced out the massive building's proportions and helped solidify the "information refinery" idea—a combination of the city's image as a stronghold for progressive technology and the state's oil and gas heritage—that weaves throughout The Webb @ LBJ. The sloped slices of the roof cylinders, which bear a loose resemblance to oil storage tanks or stacks of disks, are attention catchers and suggest to viewers that much more lies within. Further representative of the architectural marriage of old and new, the original masonry work was penetrated by new ribbons of glass, bringing natural light into the once dark interiors.

To give the single-story structure an instant vertical boost and distinct primary entry points, the architects specified the addition of 30-foot-tall as-cast concrete pylons with supporting curved composite-metal canopies. The previously bare site was extensively landscaped using concentric zones of detail. The nearer to the building one gets, the more dramatically landscaped and hardscaped it becomes, creating a certain importance about the structure and a pleasing sense of welcome for those who interact with it.

ABOVE LEFT: A minimalist approach to the renovation employs repetitive elements to define primary areas of interests.
Photograph by Steven Vaughan Photography

ABOVE RIGHT: On the west side of the building, a reflective glass façade, composite metal addition and signature concrete pylons announce the main entry.
Photograph by Steven Vaughan Photography

FACING PAGE TOP: Sloped composite metal cylinders adorn the roof, providing pure organizational geometry while enclosing all rooftop mechanical equipment.
Photograph by Steven Vaughan Photography

FACING PAGE BOTTOM: The renovated building's composition of forms is easily understood from the adjacent interstate highway, whether driving 70 miles per hour or inching along during rush hour traffic.
Photograph by Steven Vaughan Photography

Although The Webb @ LBJ was not designed for the purpose of gaining accreditation for its sustainability, the modest budget and architects' conscientiousness and creativity took the gray field project in that direction. Existing asphalt was crushed, reconstituted and used as the parking lot's base; bricks were salvaged and re-laid; and the steel was sourced from within 100 miles of the site. As the building's extensive renovation neared completion, its appellation became a point of debate, but the principal's idea for something memorable that would tell its story soon won out in popularity, and the 29-acre property was reborn as The Webb @ LBJ. ▪ ▪ ▪ ▪ ▪ ▪ ▪ ▪ ▪ ▪ ▪

White Rock Dental Group

■ ■

Azimuth : Architecture, Inc.

■ ■ ■ ■ ■ ■ ■ ■ ■ ■ ■ White Rock Dental Group's founder, Dr. Edward Lutz, commissioned Azimuth Architecture to help him balance the sleek, sterile environment necessary for a healthcare facility with a soothing, upscale design that he knew would resonate with his patients and set the tone for pleasant dental experiences.

An elegant blend of classic and modern styles, the exterior façade is clad in Texas limestone, a nod to the nearby Dallas Arboretum's regional vernacular and a conscious decision to establish a fresh, sophisticated language for the older east Dallas community on the brink of revitalization.

ABOVE: A blend of classic and modern styles, the building establishes a fresh, sophisticated language for the coming neighborhood revitalization.
Rendering by Ryan Tharel, Azimuth : Architecture, Inc.

FACING PAGE: The exterior expresses the Texas vernacular through the use of regional, natural materials, including local brick and stone as well as touches of cedar.
Project Design Team: John Taylor, Amy Shacklett and Ryan Tharel.
Photograph by James F. Wilson

One side of the building has a traditional, hip-style roof while the other has a decidedly contemporary flavor with a clean-lined stone accent wall. Traversing the elevation, the steel-canopied entrance is a throwback to historic, beamed construction, but has been reinterpreted for the building's context. The entrance's steel canopy was scaled down to a modest seven-foot height, creating a defined sense of arrival as well as a more climactic effect upon entering the interior with its unassuming nine-foot ceilings.

In response to the site's close proximity to the street, clever architectural measures were taken to minimize traffic noise as well as ensure serene vistas from within. From the dental hygienist's operatory, a wall of Austin stone that wraps around from the rear of the building serves also as a visual backdrop for the water feature and landscaping. This wall stands three feet away from the building and serves as a buffer to the street. Thoughtful window placement benefits the entire interior, bathing it in natural light.

This incredible warmth—created by sunlight and enhanced with sand-colored wall coverings and the beautiful highs and lows of Sapele wood—is juxtaposed with cool materials like the blue, mosaic-like textural carpeting, slate, brushed aluminum and frosted glass. Overall, the palette exudes an earthy yet contemporary sense of calm, inspired in part by the formal serenity of the nearby botanical gardens. Pushing the boundaries of finishes traditionally specified for health care facilities, the Azimuth team chose vinyl plank flooring that meets cleanliness requirements, looks amazingly natural and even dampens sound.

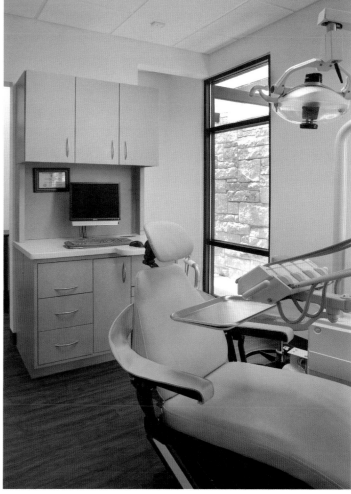

White Rock Dental Group has a welcoming exterior and a friendly interior design; the connection between these spaces is equally appropriate. As patients step into the waiting area, the angular wall immediately draws them to the reception desk and over to the seating area. Through careful, creative planning, the 3,600-square-foot facility feels much larger. Dr. Lutz was able to lease part of the space to a complementary practice until his practice required the full square footage for expansion. Clients of Azimuth have often joked that the architects have a crystal ball hidden in their studio because they always seem to know exactly what is needed to create successful spaces that accommodate current and future needs. The White Rock facility was especially rewarding in this regard, not only for the splendid architectural results but also because of the positive response from the client, staff and patients. ■ ■ ■ ■ ■ ■ ■ ■ ■ ■ ■

ABOVE LEFT: The angular waiting room draws patients to the Sapele wood and frosted glass reception desk and over to the seating area.
Photograph by James F. Wilson

ABOVE RIGHT: The interior design palette balances warm and cool materials and finishes; it expands the traditional boundaries of finishes in healthcare facilities.
Photograph by James F. Wilson

FACING PAGE: Wrapping one corner of the building, the stone accent wall provides separation from the street and serves as a backdrop to the landscaping and water feature.
Photograph by James F. Wilson

CHAPTER FIVE
Sustaining Growth

The Great Law of The Iroquois Confederacy states it best: "In our every deliberation, we must consider the impact of our decisions on the next seven generations."

The efforts of building design aimed at ensuring a more positive outlook for the future are evident in projects like SHW Group's Roy Lee Walker Elementary. The tenets, ideas and revelations of sustainability are nothing new: Our Earth is affected by the way we live. However, the commitment to Green building practices has grown and evolved into tangible methods, which architects are increasingly incorporating into their projects. From renewable materials to energy-conserving systems—these architects are discovering new innovations that are changing architecture's impact on our Earth. It is a passionate topic, but it is this passion for discovering and incorporating renewable resources that has brought Green design and building into the forefront today.

It is the hope of many architects that these practices will soon become commonplace in all forms of construction. Beneficial techniques that were once inconceivable are now not only possible, but affordable as well. The professionals who employ these commendable methods are eloquently lighting the way for others to follow.

Arbor Hills Nature Preserve, MESA, page 230

Arbor Hills Nature Preserve, MESA, page 230

Arbor Hills Nature Preserve
MESA

■ ■ ■ ■ ■ ■ ■ ■ ■ ■ ■ Plano's 200-acre gem of a parcel with an 80-foot change in topographic elevation was originally planned as a sports complex, but MESA instantly saw its raw beauty and potential and proposed alternate plans to city officials, including liaison Kenneth Phelps, who fully appreciated and believed in MESA's vision. Arbor Hills is a microcosm of what North Texas looked like before it was settled—blackland prairie, riparian forest and upland forest areas. The rarity of these three diverse ecosystems co-existing so closely and surviving the area's rigorous development heightened the importance of restoring the land so that it could serve as both a teaching tool and a place for recreation.

The trails of Arbor Hills Nature Preserve are gently woven into the natural topography, ensuring minimal impact on the ecosystem and providing fresh panoramas around every bend. Arbor Hills is best described as a series of experiences, not only while enjoying the meandering trails and vistas but also

FACING PAGE: Created in phase two, the Sentinel Tower overlooks the grandeur of the park.
Project Design Team: Stan Cowan, Robin McCaffrey, Mike Fraze and Fred Walters.
Photograph by Tom Jenkins

from the moment visitors turn north from Parker Road and make their way through the curvilinear parking. Its spiraling form mimics the manner in which a tornado would move across the terrain, a metaphor for man's destructive influence on the land. At the core of the parking facility, a bioswale, which collects rainwater from the sloped concrete surface and naturally filters the storm-water runoff before it recharges the groundwater table, has proven a point of intrigue for adults and children, alike.

Though a portion of the land was beyond restoration due to decades of agrarian use, MESA approached the seeming negative as an opportunity to be creative. The firm's professionals utilized the space for built elements like the parking facility, farmstead-inspired picnic shelters and silo-shaped bathrooms, giving a distinctive agrarian flavor to the design of each and even nostalgically preserving the windmill-capped cistern. To restore the blackland prairie to its original state, a grassland burn was instituted, decimating invasive plant life and allowing seeds of native species to regerminate. With its strong oaks and elms and under-story of mixed shrubbery, the upland forest required little editing other than the removal of a few species of nonnative trees with excessive hydration needs. As the interpretive signage communicates, it takes dangerously little to upset nature's delicate balance.

MESA, along with Larson Pedigo Architects, conceived of the master plan and successfully brought the first phase to life by approaching nature with humility, every step of the way. Benches sit low to the ground, allowing tall grasses to quietly envelop visitors; trails do not inconvenience the land's myriad wildlife; and the lookout tower—despite man's innate inclination to place it as the center of attention atop a hill—is perched only halfway from the base of the upland forest's slope, unobtrusively fostering panoramic views. A rarity in projects of this nature, several years after the first phase was finished, the city of Plano acquired more than 100 acres of land—as specified in the master plan—and MESA was able to fulfill the original vision in its entirety. The Burr Oak Pavilion is now complemented by the more-recently erected Sentinel Tower, creating an architectural dialogue across the park. A hallmark of MESA's portfolio, Arbor Hills was the earliest park of its kind in the area and, at the time of its development, one of only a few in the country. Its warm reception inspired other cities to attempt to follow suit. ■ ■ ■ ■ ■ ■ ■ ■ ■ ■ ■

ABOVE LEFT: The main trail bridge at Indian Creek leads to numerous panoramic vistas. Every visitable area of the preserve is enjoyed via accessible paths.
Photograph by Tom Jenkins

ABOVE RIGHT: Adjacent to the pavilion complex is the granary-inspired restroom facility, which was designed by Larson Pedigo Architects.
Photograph by Charles Smith

FACING PAGE: Looking to the south, the Sentinel Tower and the sky bridge that leads up to it overlook the Indian Creek tributary.
Photograph by Tom Jenkins

Roy Lee Walker Elementary

■■■■■■■■■■■■ ■

SHW Group, LLP

■ ■ ■ ■ ■ ■ ■ ■ ■ ■ ■ Every new concept needs a model, and in the area of Green building, Roy Lee Walker Elementary has served as just that. Constructed in 2000 and located in the McKinney Independent School District, Walker Elementary was designed around Green principles before the establishment of LEED certification.

The school, designed by SHW Group—a Dallas-based architecture firm—provides students with an enhanced learning environment and a focused awareness of the earth around them. The 68,788-square-foot school functions with a system of conservation and ecological sensitivity, reinforcing the importance of learning about and protecting the environment. Water is circulated using a traditional Texas windmill, pulling its energy from six strategically

FACING PAGE: Walker Elementary's learning courtyard extends teaching to the outdoors, beyond the walls of the school.
Project Design Team: Gary Keep, Mark Gerner, William Wadley and Michael Elmore.
Photograph by Michael Lyon

located cisterns that boast a 68,000-gallon capacity. Student garden areas, a nearby eco-pond and plentiful use of indigenous landscaping all contribute to what has become an outdoor classroom. Students observe water levels through a floor-to-ceiling rain gauge and the entire environment is designed to help students participate in the learning process.

The abundant Texas sunshine illuminates two distinctive sundials and, through the use of solar collectors, heats the school's water as well. The most important use of the sun's light, however, is to provide natural light within the interior spaces. Filtered through rooftop monitors, the sun's soft glow enhances the learning process. A weather center located within the school allows children to observe meteorological readings. All combined, this school serves as a unique didactic tool and reinforces the importance of Mother Earth's essential role in our lives.

The McKinney school district embarked on this project with a state-awarded grant for Green architectural research. Knowing this, the district foresaw the school's potential as a pioneering prototype. To say that Walker Elementary has positively influenced the community is an understatement. Today, Roy Lee Walker Elementary has inspired forward-thinking Green design throughout the city. An international retail chain selected McKinney for one of its prototypes and a major new car dealership soon followed suit. Both have employed earth-friendly principles during the design and construction process, and the city has

ABOVE LEFT: A bird's-eye view reveals daylight monitors, solar energy panels and a large working sundial.
Photograph by Michael Lyon

ABOVE RIGHT: A perspective of the building's side profile reveals striking angles, accentuated by working rainwater filtering and collection wells.
Photograph by Michael Lyon

FACING PAGE: Materials indigenous to the area are used inside and out, evidenced by the stone water cistern.
Photograph by Michael Lyon

even adopted a set of Green-friendly ordinances. However, no group has been more influenced than the children who attend Walker Elementary daily. The integral ideas of the design not only offer a stimulating atmosphere for young minds to thrive, but implements new ways of thinking about environmental preservation that will undoubtedly yield long-term effects. For them, Green living and Green learning have become a way of life. ■ ■ ■ ■ ■ ■ ■ ■ ■ ■ ■

CHAPTER SIX
City Futures

If a modern-day city sprung up through the creative genius of one architect alone—regardless of how talented he or she may be—it would pale in comparison to one that evolved over decades, even centuries, and was touched by the hands of many. The most spectacular cities in the world boast an eclectic mixture of architectural styles, from classical to contemporary, and it is the architect's prerogative to reinvent these broad genres to tailor a building's aesthetic appearance and functionality to the current and future needs of those who will interact with it on a daily basis.

A great deal of trust and communication is required for a group of people to conceptualize and develop plans for works of architecture that may not be tangibly built until many years down the road. CamargoCopeland's Dallas Homeless Assistance Center, WDG Architecture's 2727 Turtle Creek, Randall Scott Architects' Tyler Junior College Residence Hall and BOKA Powell's One Victory Park are a few illustrious examples. The collective realized visions of past architects provide an exquisite tapestry into which the masterpieces we call contemporary art may be harmoniously woven.

Enjoy these products of research, inspiration and diligence that will culminate in buildings yet to be constructed. Take a glimpse of what is yet to come through these dynamic drawings, blueprints and renderings.

Victory Tower, BOKA Powell, page 272

Dallas Cowboys Stadium, HKS, Inc., page 244

*Omni Fort Worth Hotel & Condominiums,
Hellmuth, Obata + Kassabaum (HOK), page 256*

2727 Turtle Creek

WDG Architecture, Inc.

WDG Architecture spent two years working to design precisely the right condominiums for one of the last premier sites in the already mature Turtle Creek neighborhood. WDG Architecture's design sought to provide a residence with the highest level of luxury and extraordinary detailing in one of Dallas' most prominent and desirable neighborhoods at 2727 Turtle Creek.

Commissioned by Trammel Crow Residential to master plan and design the 145-unit, 22-story structure on this unique site on Turtle Creek, WDG is crafting a transitional contemporary structure unlike any neighboring dwelling in the area. However, despite fashioning a more modern outward appearance, these high-rise condominiums retain all the formal elegance and grace associated with more traditional styles within—making it a wholly unique development in this posh community.

FACING PAGE: The residences at 2727 Turtle Creek combine the elegance and sophistication of traditional condominiums in a sublime contemporary structure.
Project Design Team: Jamie Fernandez-Duran, Jose Alfaro, Sanjana Dhruv and Albert Borland.
Rendering by WDG

With its contemporary exterior, condominiums are designed with spacious floorplans, vestibules, sizeable kitchens and formal living and dining rooms. Sophisticated interiors are replete with such stately elements as natural stone, choice solid-wood floors and high-end European appliances and appointments. Floor-to-ceiling glass exhibited by the contemporary structure provides an abundance of light to the formal spaces, as new owners are dazzled by brilliant downtown views while enjoying the adjacent Turtle Creek Park.

In an effort to establish a dialogue inside and out, very ample balconies and terraces serve to further enhance the interactivity with the locale's enchanting outdoor elements, supplying residents with generous outdoor living spaces comfortable for outdoor entertaining.

Catered to an affluent empty-nest owner, 2727 Turtle Creek affords buyers the opportunity to enjoy all the amenities and security features typically associated with an opulent hotel—immaculate, expansive lobbies, a large dining room for private parties, a library, concierges and ample guest services—in the comfort of a private residence.

2727 Turtle Creek is a formal space in a contemporary setting with spectacular views of the downtown skyline. WDG effectively combined its vast experience creating traditional elegant spaces in a modern structure unlike anything recently seen in Turtle Creek. ■ ■ ■ ■ ■ ■ ■ ■ ■ ■ ■

LEFT: Floor-to-ceiling glass, in addition to ample balconies and terraces, infuses interior spaces with natural light and provides brilliant views of downtown Dallas and the adjacent Turtle Creek Park.
Rendering by M2 Studio

FACING PAGE: The 22-story structure at 2727 Turtle Creek combines the amenities and security features of an opulent hotel in the comfort of a private residence.
Rendering by WDG

243

Dallas Cowboys Stadium

■■■■■■■■■■■■■■■■■■■■■■■■■■■■■■■■■■■

HKS, Inc.

■■■■■■■■■■ When Dallas Cowboys owner Jerry Jones decided to build a new stadium for his world-renowned football team, he envisioned a structure that was event-flexible, high-capacity, architecturally innovative and unique, and more than anything, a fitting home for such an iconic, storied franchise. After holding a national design competition, which was followed by presentations of preliminary design concepts and a series of interviews, HKS was selected to tackle the extraordinarily ambitious, 2.3 million-square-foot project that is unmatched in scope by any other similar venue.

One of the first requirements that Jones had for his new facility was to maintain the trademark roof opening that has characterized Texas Stadium, the team's home since 1971. However, unlike Texas Stadium's roof opening, the new stadium in Arlington will feature a retractable roof, making those early-

season games and other mid-year events held there significantly more bearable during North Texas' heat waves.

A patron to the new Cowboys stadium will immediately notice the pair of quarter-mile-long ground trusses that extend across the length of the stadium. The longest ground span trusses in the world, these two monumental elements are equal in length to the Empire State Building turned on its side. Powerful and unique in their own right, these two trusses also function as the main structural components extending over the playing field, thus enabling them to support the largest high-definition video boards of any NFL stadium.

Cognizant that its main competition was a football fan watching a 50-inch, plasma television screen from 12 feet away, HKS conducted extensive studies to replicate that football-viewing experience. The result was a pair of 180-foot-long by 50-foot-wide video boards that face each sideline. Essentially, patrons to the new Cowboys stadium in Arlington can be confident that the view they are enjoying from their seat is every bit as good—if not demonstrably better—than anything they could replicate at home.

TOP LEFT: Cowboys fans will be captivated by a one-of-a-kind feature unlike any in the world, a center-hung video board.
Rendering courtesy of HKS, Inc.

BOTTOM LEFT: The end zones feature the largest retractable doors in the world. Each has a five-leaf, translucent retractable opening measuring 120 feet high.
Rendering courtesy of HKS, Inc.

Other innovative features of the new stadium include: six paneled doors in each end zone that are equal in size to a 10-story building, look down upon large, entry plaza areas and open up completely to the outside to accommodate agreeable weather; playing field-level luxury suites that will practically position fans on the sidelines; and an 86-foot-high canted glass wall that sweeps across the venue's elegant exterior skin.

With a normal capacity of 80,000 patrons, the new stadium is also exceptionally flexible, allowing for capacities well over 100,000 for special events, like the Super Bowl, which will be held at the new stadium in 2011. The facility is right on schedule to open for the Cowboys' 2009 regular season, and thanks to Jerry Jones' grand vision combined with the practical genius employed by HKS, the new Cowboys stadium will be a grandiose facility, fitting of America's team and unparalleled by any other stadium anywhere in the world. ■ ■ ■ ■ ■ ■ ■ ■ ■ ■

ABOVE LEFT: The Cowboys' locker room is an all-inclusive destination fitted with custom wood lockers, ceiling-recessed projectors and a video display wall.
Rendering courtesy of HKS, Inc.

ABOVE RIGHT: Two silver-level clubs, at 39,000 square feet each, provide a sophisticated environment with custom detailing.
Rendering courtesy of HKS, Inc.

Dallas Homeless Assistance Center

CamargoCopeland Architects, LLP

As sunlight suffuses the Dallas Homeless Assistance Center's translucent skin, window expanses and art glass installation panels, a meditative ambience—one of well-being, peace and hope—will be instantly created. In support of their goals for the project, CamargoCopeland Architects and Overland Partners incorporated the use of translucent panels to infuse the space with natural daylight while providing privacy and outwardly expressing the residential components of the center. Working with California artist Gordon Huether, the architects successfully allowed the incorporation of public art into the architectural solution of the project, enriching the quality of the users' environment. Gleaning inspiration from journal entries submitted by previously displaced individuals, the artist created powerful, three-dimensional statements, which will be beautifully incorporated into the architectural expression of the building. The exterior and interior architecture will set the facility's tone of welcome, bolstering the organization's

ABOVE: The front façade illustrates the juxtaposition of translucent fiberglass panels and masonry, defining the housing components of the facility.
Rendering by Overland Partners

FACING PAGE: The courtyard, anchored by a communal dining room, provides a serene and humanizing space for the Dallas Homeless Assistance center's clientele.
Rendering by Jim Arp

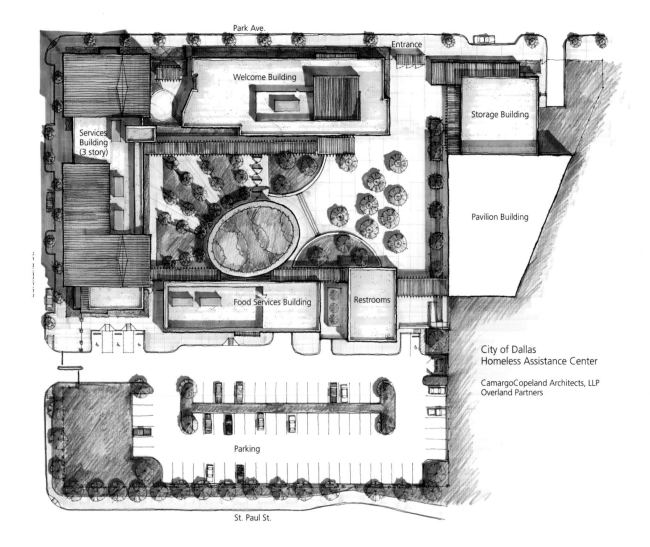

Park Ave.

Entrance

Welcome Building

Storage Building

Services
Building
(3 story)

Pavilion Building

Food Services Building

Restrooms

City of Dallas
Homeless Assistance Center

CamargoCopeland Architects, LLP
Overland Partners

Parking

St. Paul St.

efforts to not only provide a good night's rest and a nutritious meal, but also to help willing parties become self-sustaining members of society.

Low-scale and anything but threatening, the architectural composition utilizes clean lines and simple, straightforward materials like glass, masonry and brick, which mesh well with the urban fabric in the downtown neighborhood. The mingling of interior and exterior volumes is due largely to the programmatic need to serve two distinct groups: those who seek help and the chronic homeless who resist change but still require the services provided at the center. Cleverly conceived, the architectural design will manifest itself as a secure facility that also maintains the feel of a hospitable environment—as opposed to a more anonymous institutional-like setting—in which people will feel dignified.

Many basic programs—including mental and physical health, social and legal services, job training and residential services—will be offered. Because of the city's "flexibility" requirement and the architects' foresight, the Homeless Assistance Center's design was conceived with future evolutions in mind, so the architecture can easily be retrofitted or expanded as the city deems necessary.

Though the city of Dallas required that the structure achieve LEED Silver certification, the architects' goal for the project was to incorporate as many sustainable and energy-efficient design elements as creatively as possible.

ABOVE: *The service building's translucent panels glow at night, reinforcing the center's mission as a beacon of hope.*
Rendering by Jim Arp

FACING PAGE: *The architects transformed the 4.2-acre site by grouping the buildings to create manageable spaces and reinforce the urban fabric. The oversized parking remains available for future development.*
Rendering by Roberto E. Diaz, Assoc AIA, CamargoCopeland Architects

Knowing that LEED points would not be earned through building envelope energy efficiency, due to the need for the profusion of daylight and the need to expand the programmatic spaces into separate low-scale buildings, the architects implemented elements such as low-E glass and a vegetated roof over the dining hall. As well, they incorporated a gray water system, in which shower/laundry facility water and air conditioner condensation are collected, treated and reused for irrigation and flushing the large number of plumbing fixtures.

The design solution and architectural expression for the Dallas Homeless Assistance Center combine for what will undoubtedly be a successful and uplifting environment. While serving its intended demographic, the structure will also be enjoyed by casual passersby as the training center was designed to open up onto the street level to lend synergy for the users' benefit and make the center's activities evident as its residents take positive steps toward becoming self sufficient and being productive citizens. ▪ ▪ ▪ ▪ ▪ ▪ ▪ ▪ ▪ ▪ ▪

Edwards Ranch

■ ■

Looney Ricks Kiss Architects, Inc.

■ ■ ■ ■ ■ ■ ■ ■ ■ ■ ■   Established in 1848, Edwards Ranch has been a family-owned enterprise for nearly 160 years, and six generations of Edwards have cultivated its rich soil and herded cattle across its plains. At present, the Edwards family, as Cassco Land, is developing the final remnant of its once 7,000-plus-acre family ranch with Isaac Manning of Trinity Works as co-developer. With this 850-acre expanse along the Trinity River—the lone undeveloped property along the Trinity inside the core of Fort Worth, the family hopes to leave a lasting legacy that will shape the future development of Fort Worth, reconnect the city and its residents with the river and set a new standard for urban design.

Enlisting the services of Looney Ricks Kiss Architects, the Edwards family and Manning entrusted LRK with the grand task of crafting a vision for the remaining property and creating an enduring destination for Fort Worth. LRK developed design guidelines to strengthen and define the

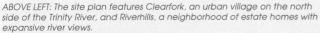

ABOVE LEFT: The site plan features Clearfork, an urban village on the north side of the Trinity River, and Riverhills, a neighborhood of estate homes with expansive river views.
Image courtesy of Looney Ricks Kiss Architects, Inc.

ABOVE RIGHT: As one of the last pieces of undeveloped land in close proximity to the heart of Fort Worth, the Edwards family felt a civic duty to preserve this corridor.
Image courtesy of Looney Ricks Kiss Architects, Inc.

FACING PAGE: With a mix of land uses and building densities, the village center of Clearfork is designed to integrate varied aspects of daily life.
Rendering by Phil Hamilton

family's vision, based on urban design criteria fashioned from the firm's extensive experience with similar projects across the United States and internationally.

Harkening back to a pre-World War II tradition, LRK encapsulated the rich, communal neighborhood atmosphere that permeated communities of that era. Capturing the "DNA" of those earlier settlements, the design team laid out the Riverhills Neighborhood so that houses favorably relate to one another and the streets—creating a sense of place for its inhabitants. Clearfork, the planned town center for Edwards Ranch, will feature a diverse offering of commercial properties in addition to some denser, multifamily residences. Moreover, the southern frontage for Clearfork Town Center runs along the Trinity, animating the adjacent street that hugs the river and engaging the town center—perpendicular streets connect to the "riverside drive," offering picturesque views throughout the town center—to create a façade for the city on the river.

Utilizing the dynamic natural resources afforded by this terrain in a responsible way was imperative to the Edwards family and faithfully executed by the project team. To preserve the area's mature trees—some of which are older than Edwards Ranch itself—LRK integrated open spaces and park systems, and further minimized impact with lightly structured street designs and sensitive exterior materials for residences. Paths and walkways connect various elements throughout the development and lead to the Trinity Trail, further engendering the simpler neighborhood atmospheres of another generation.

As conceived by the planning team at Looney Ricks Kiss, the mixed-use development at Edwards Ranch will provide a vibrant model for the city's future development while furthering a lasting legacy for the Edwards family. ■ ■ ■ ■ ■ ■ ■ ■ ■ ■ ■

Omni Fort Worth Hotel & Condominiums

■ ■

Hellmuth, Obata + Kassabaum (HOK)

■ ■ ■ ■ ■ ■ ■ ■ ■ ■ The Omni Fort Worth Hotel & Condominiums represents a bold mixed-use development in the heart of Fort Worth, providing a flagship hotel to serve the nearby, HOK-designed and renovated convention center. The project represents the first new downtown hotel construction in more than 20 years, as well as an iconic, instantly identifiable high-rise contributing to the city's skyline. The Omni project is a dynamic combination of hotel rooms, luxury condominiums, upscale restaurants, bars and retail concepts gracefully designed by the exceptional team at HOK.

This ambitious undertaking has resulted in designs for a 33-story building containing more than 600 hotel rooms, 90 luxury condominiums and three levels of underground parking accommodating 550 vehicles. The ground level contains a vibrant, two-story, 7,000-square-foot hotel lobby and gracious porte

FACING PAGE: The Omni Fort Worth Hotel & Condominiums is depicted within its urban context, which includes the adjacent Fort Worth Convention Center, recently renovated and expanded by HOK.
Project Design Team: Bill Hellmuth, Steven Janeway, Kirk Millican, Stephen Brookover and Javier Espinoza.
Rendering by Dariush Vaziri

cochere. The grand lobby is designed to open up at street level, making the many retail concepts being planned for this elegant space accessible to the urban fabric outside the hotel. This ample lobby area is intended to symbolize a veritable living room for downtown Fort Worth.

In addition to the ground floor presence of a sports bar, coffee shop, Omni concept restaurant, steak and chop specialty restaurant, wine bar and gift shop, there is a separate entrance and lobby for the condominium units. One level above the street, an 18,000-square-foot grand ballroom and 10,000-square-foot junior ballroom, along with their corresponding pre-function spaces, overlook the nearby Fort Worth Water Gardens and convention center, affording highly desirable social spaces for breakout functions. The third floor contains additional meeting spaces, as well as the hotel's spa, fitness center, and outdoor pool. Viewed in combination, the banquet, meeting and pre-function spaces total more than 65,000 square feet.

Atop the two-block hotel podium rest 12 floors of hotel rooms. The plan of the hotel room floors is designed in the shape of an "L," with vertical circulation at the center, to truncate the corridors' length. The luxury condominiums begin at the 16th floor with a separate fitness facility, pool and party area. The condominium floors are smaller in size than the hotel and comprise five distinct units, each with its own balcony. The 17 stories of condo units are draped in a high-performance glass curtain-wall system elongated with vertically expressed

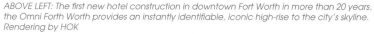

ABOVE LEFT: The first new hotel construction in downtown Fort Worth in more than 20 years, the Omni Forth Worth provides an instantly identifiable, iconic high-rise to the city's skyline.
Rendering by HOK

ABOVE RIGHT: The dynamic structure's exterior is comprised of copious glass along with native hardwoods and natural stone, fomenting a distinct style respective of its architectural vernacular.
Rendering by HOK

FACING PAGE: Seventeen stories of condominiums begin on the 16th floor, and the units are encased in a high-performance, glass curtain-wall system elongated with vertically expressed, exterior mullions.
Rendering by M2 Studio

exterior mullions. The curtain-wall segments the hotel room block, using its continuous progression through the larger structure to define the condominium entrance at the street. The prominent vertical mullions of the building skin further emphasize the tower's expansive vertical scale while partially shading the glass along the western and eastern façades from extreme sun.

Distinctive for its unique structure and immense dimensions, the 485-foot, mixed-use building's exterior will feature a variety of materials, such as hardwoods and natural stone, engendering a distinct style that is respectful of its urban context. Deftly designed by HOK, the Omni Fort Worth Hotel & Condominiums is sure to be an extraordinary, must-visit destination for any and all visiting Fort Worth. ■ ■ ■ ■ ■ ■ ■ ■ ■ ■ ■

One Victory Park

■ ■

BOKA Powell

■ ■ ■ ■ ■ ■ ■ ■ ■ ■ Embodying Dallas' first master-planned community in which public space is an integral part of the overall planned concept, Victory Park is the perfect fusion of public spaces and mixed uses supported by pedestrian and livable environments. An integral part of this burgeoning development, One Victory Park epitomizes the future of urban office development.

One Victory Park is the first of a pair of adjacent buildings that front the 1.5-acre Victory Park—an inviting and dynamic location within the larger 75-acre development that teems with energy and activity—and represents a pertinent component of an area characterized by wide sidewalks, narrow streets and large public venues. Both towers consist primarily of class-A office space that rests on a first-floor retail base. The lower-level retail interacts brilliantly

FACING PAGE: A pair of adjacent towers fronting Victory Park, these mixed-use structures feature expansive, class-A office space and first-floor retail in a vibrant urban setting.
Rendering courtesy of BOKA Powell

with the adjacent park grounds. Planned restaurants and coffee shops will allow patrons to enjoy bistro table seating in the park, or lounge in the active sidewalk environment, as well as provide office workers with appealing leisure areas.

The office buildings, which are LEED-accredited Silver, are highly flexible, carefully crafted structures. Planned largely from the inside-out, the buildings' space planning drove the floor shape, which was envisioned to be the optimal law firm floor plate. Planned according to a five-foot grid that engenders maximum flexibility for perimeter offices, the buildings utilize sawtooth corners that allow for eight uniform corner offices, rather than the typical four.

Moreover, the office spaces feature an unprecedented under-floor air distribution system, which gives each person individual air-conditioning control in his or her personal space. Access flooring also allows for total plug-and-play flexibility for

under-floor telephone, power and data distribution. Collectively, these elements provide tenants with maximum flexibility to space plan their office as their particular needs require.

One Victory Park also includes a seven-story parking garage and a high-end motor court that provides a functional yet distinguished entry sequence. The entry court interacts well with the park as it addresses its corner, providing an optimal place to cross the street to the park grounds. An integral element of the bold plan envisaged for the Victory Park development, One Victory Park is the product of the adroit planning and implementation that characterizes the dynamic work of BOKA Powell.

ABOVE LEFT: The grand ground-level lobby's first-floor retail, restaurants, coffee shops and the park create an active and engaging urban environment in which these office towers are located.
Rendering courtesy of BOKA Powell

ABOVE RIGHT: The buildings are LEED Silver certified, and office space is highly flexible thanks to plug-and-play access flooring, an under-floor air distribution system and optimal floor plates.
Rendering courtesy of BOKA Powell

FACING PAGE: One Victory Park, along with the nearby W Hotel and other Victory development, is redefining the Dallas skyline.
Rendering courtesy of BOKA Powell

SHW Group
North Texas Studio / Corporate Office

■ ■

SHW Group

■ ■ ■ ■ ■ ■ ■ ■ ■ ■ SHW Group, one of the nation's top educational design architects, creates innovative, inspiring learning environments. It seems natural then that its company headquarters and North Texas office offer staff an equally inspiring atmosphere. Legacy Town Center—a work/live/shop community in Plano—will be the new home for SHW Group, placing the company in a vibrant social and residential setting. Here, the team has designed not only a new work space, but an entirely new way of conducting business that is a culture unto itself.

With Green principles in mind, SHW Group has incorporated eco-friendly features into the space and in how the firm operates—an approach that translates to the work the architects produce for clients and how they work each day. That higher quality of life has led to a system of employee management unique to SHW Group's North Texas studio. The group decided to replace in-house departmental and seniority-based segregation with, what they call,

FACING PAGE: A glass cube appears to float above the space, serving as the office's central conference room and symbolizing the firm's untethered potential.
Project Design Team: Gary Keep, Mark E. Gerner, Jimmy Strohmeyer, Konrad Judd, Michael Hall, Jonathan Aldis, Dale Bitting and Megan Howie.
Rendering by J.Ehler, V.Lazar, AIA - SHW Group, North Texas

neighborhoods. Fourteen annually rotating neighborhoods are comprised of eight people with various backgrounds and specialties, looking to each other for collaboration, connection and support. This promotes an egalitarian, kinetic environment where ideas expand and build upon one another.

The physical arrangement of the space furthers this flat company hierarchy concept by removing enclosed offices and cubicles. Office location no longer indicates rank, refusing preferential treatment to even Gary Keep, the firm's chief executive officer. A meandering trail connects the open neighborhoods, journeying through spaces that can be manipulated to adapt with group innovations and ideas. This also creates the opportunity for open communication, sporadic meetings and the overall enhancement of teamwork.

The space veers far from stereotypically stifling corporate atmospheres, with sunlight and window visibility that will reach 90 percent of team members throughout their workday. By functioning as a paperless society, the space-consuming products will be removed, offering staff and clients more room to discover and experiment with new features for future educational projects. Visitors and employees

will be empowered to connect in both a visual and tactile way with prospective designs, materials and lighting techniques. Demonstrations and philosophies will come to life in what is set up to be an interactive, living laboratory.

The distinctive office layout was unveiled to the staff via a collaborative poem which, like the space, has a set structure, where each piece is weighted with meaning—a Shakespearean sonnet. The verse is proudly posted outside of an elevated conference room, the central element of the new office. Perched as a beacon to SHW Group's designs, the raised plane mysteriously floats above the rest of the office, symbolizing the company's inventive, untethered potential. ■ ■ ■ ■ ■ ■ ■ ■ ■ ■

ABOVE LEFT: The office spills out into public space, engaging both guests and staff members before they enter.
Rendering by J.Ehler, V.Lazar AIA - SHW Group, North Texas

ABOVE RIGHT: Open, collaborative, "neighborhood" work spaces are joined by a meandering path.
Rendering by J.Ehler, V.Lazar AIA - SHW Group, North Texas

FACING PAGE: The reception area—defined by an outreaching, floating plane—doubles as a gallery showcasing the firm's work.
Rendering by J.Ehler, V.Lazar AIA - SHW Group, North Texas

Tyler Junior College Residence Hall

Randall Scott Architects, Inc.

■ ■ ■ ■ ■ ■ ■ ■ ■ ■ ■ Tyler Junior College commissioned Randall Scott Architects, a leading designer of student housing in the southern United States, to create a signature residence hall and commons building embodying the campus's Georgian Colonial architectural heritage, which the college wanted to reinstate after several decades of eclectic design.

Given that the project site was at the lowest elevation on campus and was bisected by an indigenous creek with significant portions of the site in an unusable flood plain, RSA's design called for two limited-footprint, four-story residence towers paralleling the axis of the creek and taking advantage of the natural vistas. Circulation between the towers occurs along two 100-foot-long, clear-span white tubular steel pedestrian bridges with exposed wood

FACING PAGE: Red brick, white cast stone accents, gabled pediments, pitched roofs, white cornices, multi-light windows and four-story limestone columns collectively embody the intended Georgian Colonial style.
Project Design Team: Randall B. Scott and Gregory J. Conaway.
Rendering courtesy of Randall Scott Architects, Inc.

canopies, allowing students to experience the aromas and sounds wafting from the native creek below and the solid canopy of hardwoods above.

The exterior of the building was adroitly composed of traditional Georgian Colonial elements of red brick, white cast stone accents, large white cornices, gabled pediments, pitched roofs, multi-light windows and four-story limestone columns. Designed as a recruiting and retention tool for the college, residents enter the residence hall into an expansive two-story atrium replete with inviting wood-paneled walls and columns, granite floors with carpet inlays, brass sconces, a 30-foot-tall brick accent wall and a stainless steel chandelier. A second-floor bridge spans the atrium overlooking the front entrance lobby on the west and the student lounge to the east, providing opportunities for student interaction.

Creating student interaction opportunities for today's millennium-generation students was paramount in the minds of the residence life staff at TJC and RSA. To foster communal interactivity among residents, the design team created large verandas, adjacent to the residence life towers on each side of the creek, which descend toward the water's edge, allowing students to experience nature while studying or just taking a break from the everyday demands of college life. To reintegrate today's reclusive, internet-

immersed students, the design team created a cyber lounge—a high-tech messaging, entertainment and communal gaming environment for students enthralled with the internet, located adjacent to the main student lounge. Additional student amenities include a computer room, billiards room, convenience store, club meeting room and a large, well-appointed meeting room with a catering kitchen.

Embracing opportunities for "campus life" in a signature building eschewing the architectural roots of the TJC campus, this new residence hall overwhelmingly captures the owner's desire for a signature 100-year building while enveloping a native oasis for student rejuvenation. ■ ■ ■ ■ ■ ■ ■ ■ ■ ■ ■

ABOVE LEFT: The residence hall's inviting, two-story atrium incorporates such refined elements as wood-paneled walls and columns, granite floors with carpet inlays, brass sconces, a 30-foot-tall brick accent wall and a stainless steel chandelier.
Rendering courtesy of Randall Scott Architects, Inc.

ABOVE RIGHT: The cyber lounge, a high-tech entertainment, messaging and communal gaming environment for reclusive, internet-immersed students, provides opportunities for social interaction among an often isolated sector of the student body.
Rendering courtesy of Randall Scott Architects, Inc.

FACING PAGE: Circulation between the two residence halls is facilitated by a pair of 100-foot-long, clear-span white tubular steel pedestrian bridges with exposed wood canopies, which allow students to enjoy the ambient sights, sounds and smells of the native creek below.
Rendering courtesy of Randall Scott Architects, Inc.

Victory Tower

■ ■

BOKA Powell

■ ■ ■ ■ ■ ■ ■ ■ ■ ■ Victory Park represents the ultimate in master-planned, mixed-use urban development. Located in the heart of downtown, Victory Tower will stand above all neighboring structures as the defining building in the 21st-century Dallas skyline—an icon that will instantly be associated with the city of Dallas.

Commissioned by Victory Park developer Hillwood, BOKA Powell initially established the program elements in a template document for this exceptionally ambitious undertaking. New York's Kohn Peterson Fox was commissioned as the design architect. As the architect of record, BOKA Powell will be responsible for overseeing and ensuring consistent progress on this massive endeavor, collaborating with KPF throughout the design process.

FACING PAGE: At 46 stories tall and literally five inches away from the FAA's maximum allowable building height, Victory Tower eclipses all other Victory Park developments. Rendering by Crystal CG

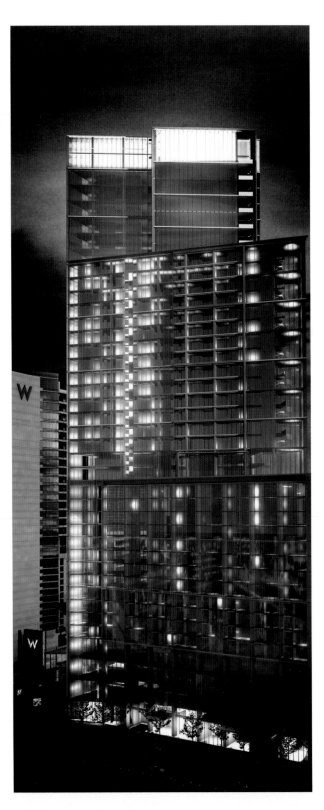

A 46-story building, Victory Tower will incorporate a variety of well-defined uses, the cornerstone of which is an upscale Mandarin Oriental Hotel. The tower's first 12 floors will consist primarily of Mandarin hotel rooms, including approximately 150 luxury guestrooms and an amenity floor featuring an outdoor podium with a pool deck and spa. The next eight floors feature 230,000 square feet of highly efficient, cutting-edge office space, which are followed by 16 floors of luxury condominiums that will be serviced by the Mandarin. The final six floors will feature unfinished luxury penthouses, allowing a select group of owners to bring in their own designers and personalize their luxurious abodes.

Deft patterning and varying exterior elements serve to distinguish the different uses, including the variation of floor heights, separate and distinct massing and prominent balconies at the residential floors. Thanks to a skewed floor plan that deviates slightly from the grid on which downtown Dallas is established, all views relate to the city's existing urban landscape, providing optimal vistas throughout the tower.

In addition to boldly redefining the Dallas skyline, Victory Tower incorporates numerous sustainable design elements. The tower's high-performance glass skin maximizes visible light inside while expelling heat. Moreover, roof gardens and pool decks atop Victory Tower combat the heat island effect associated with most tall urban structures. Unlike the concrete roof slabs that characterize most

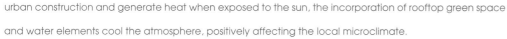

urban construction and generate heat when exposed to the sun, the incorporation of rooftop green space and water elements cool the atmosphere, positively affecting the local microclimate.

An iconic and multifaceted structure, Victory Tower will forever alter the Dallas skyline, ushering in a new era of dynamic mixed-use construction. At 46 stories tall, the tower will transcend all other Victory Park development and is the result of the prescient planning and progressive vision employed by BOKA Powell and KPF. ■ ■ ■ ■ ■ ■ ■ ■ ■ ■ ■

ABOVE LEFT: This boldly ambitious undertaking will consist primarily of 12 floors of five-star Mandarin Oriental Hotel rooms, eight floors of rentable office space, 16 floors of pre-finished luxury condominiums and six floors of opulent penthouses.
Rendering by Crystal CG

ABOVE RIGHT: Victory Tower's site orientation is skewed towards downtown Dallas, taking advantage of the resplendent views in this burgeoning urban area.
Rendering by Crystal CG

FACING PAGE LEFT: A view from Olive Street at dusk. The building's layering effectively expresses specific program elements in this vibrant, mixed-use high-rise.
Rendering by Crystal CG

FACING PAGE RIGHT: The tower's high-performance glass skin infuses interiors with light while expelling heat. Roof gardens and pool decks help mitigate the heat island effect typically associated with tall urban structures.
Rendering by BOKA Powell

PUBLISHING TEAM

Brian G. Carabet, Publisher
John A. Shand, Publisher
Steve Darocy, Executive Publisher
Martha Cox, Senior Associate Publisher
Karla Setser, Senior Associate Publisher

Beth Benton, Director of Development & Design
Julia Hoover, Director of Book Marketing & Distribution
Elizabeth Gionta, Editorial Development Specialist

Michele Cunningham-Scott, Art Director
Emily Kattan, Senior Graphic Designer
Ben Quintanilla, Senior Graphic Designer
Jonathan Fehr, Graphic Designer
Ashley Rodges, Graphic Designer

Rosalie Z. Wilson, Managing Editor
Katrina Autem, Editor
Amanda Bray, Editor
Lauren Castelli, Editor
Anita M. Kasmar, Editor
Ryan Parr, Editor
Daniel Reid, Editor

Kristy Randall, Managing Production Coordinator
Laura Greenwood, Production Coordinator
Jennifer Lenhart, Production Coordinator
Jessica Adams, Traffic Coordinator

Carol Kendall, Administrative Manager
Beverly Smith, Administrative Assistant
Amanda Mathers, Sales Support Coordinator

PANACHE PARTNERS, LLC
CORPORATE OFFICE
1424 Gables Court
Plano, TX 75075
469.246.6060
www.panache.com

DALLAS OFFICE
Martha Cox 972.966.6169
Karla Setser 214.437.3950

THE PANACHE COLLECTION

Dream Homes Series

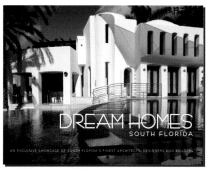

Dream Homes of Texas
Dream Homes South Florida
Dream Homes Colorado
Dream Homes Metro New York
Dream Homes Greater Philadelphia
Dream Homes New Jersey
Dream Homes Florida
Dream Homes Southwest
Dream Homes Northern California
Dream Homes Carolinas
Dream Homes Georgia
Dream Homes Chicago
Dream Homes Southern California
Dream Homes Washington, D.C.
Dream Homes Deserts
Dream Homes Pacific Northwest
Dream Homes Minnesota
Dream Homes Ohio & Pennsylvania
Dream Homes California Central Coast
Dream Homes New England
Dream Homes Los Angeles
Dream Homes Michigan
Dream Homes Tennessee

Additional Titles

Spectacular Hotels
Spectacular Golf of Texas
Spectacular Golf of Colorado
Spectacular Restaurants of Texas
Elite Portfolios
Spectacular Wineries of Napa Valley

City by Design Series

City by Design Dallas
City by Design Atlanta
City by Design San Francisco Bay Area
City by Design Pittsburgh
City by Design Chicago
City by Design Charlotte
City by Design Phoenix, Tucson & Albuquerque
City by Design Denver
City by Design Orlando
City by Design Los Angeles

Perspectives on Design Series

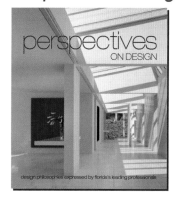

Perspectives on Design Florida
Perspectives on Design Georgia
Perspectives on Design New England

Spectacular Homes Series

Spectacular Homes of Texas
Spectacular Homes of Georgia
Spectacular Homes of South Florida
Spectacular Homes of Tennessee
Spectacular Homes of the Pacific Northwest
Spectacular Homes of Greater Philadelphia
Spectacular Homes of the Southwest
Spectacular Homes of Colorado
Spectacular Homes of the Carolinas
Spectacular Homes of Florida
Spectacular Homes of California
Spectacular Homes of Michigan
Spectacular Homes of the Heartland
Spectacular Homes of Chicago
Spectacular Homes of Washington, D.C.
Spectacular Homes of Ohio & Pennsylvania
Spectacular Homes of Minnesota
Spectacular Homes of New England
Spectacular Homes of New York
Spectacular Homes of London

Visit www.panache.com or call
469.246.6060

PANACHE PARTNERS, LLC

Creators of Spectacular Publications for
Discerning Readers

FEATURED FIRMS

AIA Dallas
1444 Oak Lawn Avenue, Suite 600
Dallas, TX 75207
214.742.3242
www.aiadallas.org

Architecture Demarest
David T. Demarest, AIA
801 Core Street, Suite B
Dallas, TX 75207
214.748.6655
www.architecturedemarest.com
Notable Projects: The Village, Oklahoma State University;
Victory Hall, University of North Texas; Port Lawrence, Palm
Springs, CA; The Island on Lake Travis, Lago Vista, TX;
Market-Ross Place, West End, Dallas.

Azimuth : Architecture, Inc.
Jack Atkins, AIA; John Taylor
4228 North Central Expressway, Suite 100
Dallas, TX 75206
214.261.9060
www.azimutharc.com
Notable Projects: Sandy Lake 121 Business Center;
Children's Medical Center Bright Building, Moncrief
Cancer Center; Lake Vista 7 Office Center; Palm Beach
Tan Corporate Headquarters.

Beeler Guest Owens Architects, LLP
Jerrold P. Beeler; John L. Guest; John N. Owens
4245 North Central Expressway, Suite 300
Dallas, TX 75205
214.520.8878
www.bgoarchitects.com
Notable Projects: Mercantile Block, Dallas; The Dallas
Power & Light Block; Slocum Street Lofts, Dallas; The
Quarry, San Antonio; The Sanctuary, San Marcos.

BOKA Powell
Chris W. Barnes, AIA; John E. Orfield; Michael B. Kennedy,
AIA; Donald R. Powell Jr., AIA
8070 Park Lane, Suite 300
Dallas, TX 75231
972.701.9000
www.bokapowell.com
Notable Projects: Mandarin Oriental-Victory, mixed-use;
One Victory Park, office; Two Victory Park, office; Granite
Park Hotel; Granite Park IV and V.

Brown Reynolds Watford Architects, Inc.
Craig S. Reynolds, FAIA; Mark Watford, AIA, LEED AP;
Gary DeVries, AIA, LEED AP;
Lisa W. Lamkin, AIA, CSI, LEED AP
3535 Travis Street, Suite 250
Dallas, TX 75204
214.528.8704
www.brwarch.com
Dallas – College Station, TX – Houston
Notable Projects: Jack Lowe Sr. Elementary and Sam Tasby
Middle School Combined Campus; DCCCD El Centro
College West Campus; Texas A&M Systems Headquarters;
Texas Horse Park; Dallas Fire Station No. 33.

CamargoCopeland Architects, LLP
Myriam E. Camargo, AIA, LEED AP;
E.J. Copeland, AIA, NCARB
14755 Preston Road, Suite 845
Dallas, TX 75254
972.934.7600
www.camargocopeland.com
Notable Projects: Irving ISD Administrative Complex;
PNC Mortgage Company; Fogo de Chão Churrascaria;
Grimaldi's Pizzeria.

Edwin Brantley Smith & Associates, Inc.
Edwin Brantley Smith, AIA
6688 North Central Expressway, Suite 580
Dallas, TX 75206
214.368.1900
www.edwinbrantleysmith.com
Notable Projects: Mockingbird Depot, Dallas; Knox
Place, Dallas; T-Mobile USA Retail & Engineering
Facilities; Hattiesburg Lake Terrace Convention Center,
Hattiesburg, MS; Interiors of Le Cordon Bleu College of
Culinary Arts, Dallas.

F&S Partners Incorporated
G. Allen Atkinson Jr., AIA; Ronald J. Shaw, AIA;
Robert L. Shaw Jr., AIA; Anita Picozzi Moran, AIA
8350 North Central Expressway, Suite 500
Dallas, TX 75206
214.559.4851
www.fsarchitects.com
Notable Projects: J. Erik Jonsson Central Library;
UT Southwestern's Simmons Biomedical Research
Building Park; Cities Baptist Church additions; The
Women's Museum.

Gensler
Judy Pesek, IIDA, LEED AP; Cindy Simpson, IIDA, LEED AP;
Paul Manno, AIA, IIDA; Ted Kollaja, AIA, LEED AP;
Gus Hinojosa, AIA, IIDA, LEED AP
5430 LBJ Freeway
Three Lincoln Center, Suite 400
Dallas, TX 75240
214.273.1500
www.gensler.com
More than 30 locations worldwide
Notable Projects: EnCana Corporation; Hunt
Consolidated, Inc.; Mary Kay; Rosewood; HBK; Haynes
and Boone, LLP, Dallas.

Gromatzky Dupree & Associates
Charles E. Gromatzky, AIA;
Robert B. Dupree, AIA, NCARB
2626 Cole Avenue, Suite 300
Dallas, TX 75204
214.871.9078
www.gdainet.com
Dallas – Phoenix – Tucson
Notable Projects: International Center; Alliance Gateway
Industrial Park; Cirque; The Tower Residences at the The
Stoneleigh Hotel; 210 Trade.

Harry C. Hoover Jr. Architects and Planners
Harry C. Hoover Jr.
2909 Cole Avenue, Suite 302
Dallas, TX 75204
214.871.0380
Notable Projects: Burns Hacienda; 300-room hotel at
5th and Commerce in Ft. Worth; bank/office building at
Preston and Sherry Lane; Preston Hills Tennis Club; ranch
estate near Walnut Springs, TX.

Hellmuth, Obata + Kassabaum, L.P. (HOK)
Bill Prindle; Sandra Paret, AIA; Steven Janeway, AIA;
Brion Sargent, AIA; Kirk Millican, AIA
2711 North Haskell Avenue, Suite 2250, LB 26
Dallas, TX 75204
214.720.6000
www.hok.com
26 locations worldwide
Notable Projects: Exxon/ Mobil World Headquarters;
Dallas Galleria; DFW International Airport; 2100 McKinney
Office Building; North Central Expressway Urban Design.

Hensley Lamkin Rachel, Inc.
David W. Hensley, AIA, APA; Robert W. Lamkin, AIA,
NCARB; Bruce W. Rachel, AIA, NCARB, CSI
13800 Montfort Drive, Suite 310
Dallas, TX 75240
972.726.9400
www.hlrinc.net
Notable Projects: Austin Ranch Phases II and III and Dry
Creek Lodge, The Colony; SoCo Lofts and Condos, Austin;
Alexan Lofts, Houston; Alexan Skyline, Dallas; Kessler
Woods Phase III Townhomes, Dallas.

HH Architects
Jerry Halcomb, AIA, CSI; Bruce Woody, AIA;
Jones McConnell, AIA; Jim Stewart, AIA; Jim Crandell, AIA
5910 North Central Expressway, Suite 1200
Dallas, TX 75206
972.404.1034
www.hharchitects.com
Notable Projects: First Baptist Orlando Worship Center, FL;
Falls Creek Encampment Worship/Conference Center, OK;
Brentwood Baptist Deaf Worship Center, TN; Germantown
Baptist Worship Center, TN.

Hidell & Associates Architects, Inc.
William Hidell; Tony Blaas; Aaron Babcock
3033 Kellway Drive, Suite 120
Carrollton, TX 75006
972.416.4666
www.hidell.com
Notable Projects: Farmington Public Library, Farmington,
NM; Warren Civic Complex – City Hall / Library, Warren,
MI; EDS Cluster 3, Plano, TX; St. Seraphim Russian
Orthodox, Dallas.

HKS, Inc.
H. Ralph Hawkins, FAIA, FACHA; Ronald L. Skaggs, FAIA,
FACHA; Nunzio M. DeSantis, AIA; Craig Beale, FAIA,
FACHA, RIBA, CHC, CHE
1919 McKinney Avenue
Dallas, TX 75201
214.969.5599
www.hksinc.com
20 locations worldwide
Notable Projects: Las Ventanas Al Paraiso, Los Cabos,
Mexico; Liverpool Football Club Stadium, Liverpool,
England; MGM City Center Block A, Las Vegas; Children's
Hospital & Regional Medical Center, Seattle.

Hocker Design Group
David Hocker, RLA, ASLA
918 Dragon Street
Dallas, TX 75207
214.915.0910
www.hockerdesign.com

Jennings*Hackler & Partners, Inc.
Robert Hackler, AIA; Grady Jennings, AIA
4131 North Central Expressway, Suite 400
Dallas, TX 75204
214.528.8644
www.jennings-hackler.com
Notable Projects: UT Austin's Nano Science and
Technology Building; Trinity Fellowship Church; Texas
A&M's Wehner Building; Texas A&M-Commerce's Science
Building; UT Austin's Moffett Molecular Biology Building.

johnson / twitmyer
*a joint venture of Sally Johnson Architect and
Carole Twitmyer Designer*
Sally Johnson, AIA
4140 Commerce Street, Suite 101
Dallas, TX 75226
214.826.3700
www.sallyjohnsonarchitect.com
Notable Projects: Spinks Airport Terminal, Fort Worth;
Union Gospel's Center of Hope, Dallas; Temple Day Care
Center; new Prairie-style residence in Highland Park, TX.

Looney Ricks Kiss Architects, Inc.
H. Frank Ricks, AIA; Paige C. Close, AIA;
Robert B Norcross, AIA; Rebecca L. Courtney, ASID, IIDA;
G. William Belshaw, AIA, LEED AP; Howard Goldstein, AIA
5307 East Mockingbird Lane, Suite 220
Dallas, TX 75206
214.242.7650
www.lrk.com
Baton Rouge – Boulder – Celebration, FL – Dallas –
Jacksonville – Memphis – Nashville – Princeton, NJ –
Rosemary Beach, FL
Notable Projects: The Bel Air, Houston; Upper Kirby,
Houston; West Ave, Houston; Water Street-Las Colinas,
Irving; Tortuga Harbor, Padre Island.

MESA
Tary Arterburn, ASLA; Stan Cowan, ASLA; Mike Fraze,
ASLA; Fred Walters, ASLA; Chip Impastato, ASLA
1807 Ross Avenue, Suite 333
Dallas, TX 75201
214.871.0568
www.mesadesigngroup.com
Notable Projects: ReyRosa; Manuta Community;
Shangri La; Beck Park; Fellowship Youth Camp.

NCA Partners
Lance Rose; Nick Cade
12162 Abrams Road, Suite 200
Dallas, TX 75243
214.361.9901
www.ncapartners.com
Notable Projects: Covenant Church;
Faith Landmark Ministries.

Options Real Estate Development
Monte Anderson
1801 North Hampton Road, Suite 400
DeSoto, TX 75115
972.283.1111
www.optionsre.com
Notable Projects: The Enclave at Thorntree, DeSoto, TX;
Main Station Duncanville, Duncanville, TX; Fire Station
at 600 North Bishop, Dallas; mixed use at 1322 North
Beckley, Dallas.

PageSoutherlandPage
Mattia Flabiano, AIA, ACHA
3500 Maple Avenue, Suite 600
Dallas, TX 75219
214.522.3900
www.pspaec.com
Austin – Dallas – Houston – Washington, D.C.
Notable Projects: Texas Instruments, Inc., RFAB,
Richardson, TX; Children's Medical Center Legacy, Plano,
TX; The University of Texas at Dallas, NSERL Building,
Richardson, TX; Norman Regional Hospital Healthplex
Campus, Norman, OK; Cirque, Dallas, TX.

Pro·Forma Architecture, Inc.
Jeff D. Bulla III, AIA, LEED AP
17000 North Dallas Parkway, Suite 115
Dallas, TX 75248
972.713.7100
www.proforma-inc.com
Notable Projects: Anna City Hall; City of Coppell Senior
Recreation/Community Center; City of Allen Fire Station
No. 5; City of Allen Senior Recreation Center; Collin Creek
Community Church, Plano, TX.

Randall Scott Architects, Inc.
Randall B. Scott, AIA
14755 Preston Road, Suite 730
Dallas, TX 75254
972.664.9100
www.rsarchitects.com
Notable Projects: University of Mary Hardin Baylor
Convocation & Recreation Center; Haltom City Central
Fire Station; University of Texas Permian Basin Student
Housing; City of Commerce Towne Centre; North Lake
College Science Building.

Rees Associates, Inc.
Frank W. Rees Jr., AIA; Leroy James, AIA; Jan Blackmon,
FAIA; Richard Macri; Ralph Blackman, AIA
1801 North Lamar, Suite 600
Dallas, TX 75202
214.522.7337
www.rees.com
Atlanta – Dallas – Oklahoma City
Notable Projects: Anadolu Medical Center, Turkey; UNLV
Moot Court, NV; Longhorn Village CCRC, TX; West Texas
A&M University Fine Arts Complex, TX; BET Corporate
Headquarters, Washington, D.C.

Ron Hobbs Architects
Ron Hobbs, AIA
614 West Main Street, Suite 200
Garland, TX 75040
972.494.0174
www.ronhobbsarchitects.net
Notable Projects: Sunnyvale Town Hall; Hurst City Hall;
The Atrium at the Granville Arts Center, Garland; Williams
Funeral Home, Garland; Waxahachie Civic Center.

RTKL Associates, Inc.
Brad Barker, AIA, NCARB; John Castorina, AIA, ACHA;
Jeff Gunning, AIA; Tom Brink, AIA;
Todd Lundgren, AIA, NCARB
1717 Pacific Avenue
Dallas, TX 75201
214.871.8877
www.rtkl.com
Baltimore – Chicago – Dallas – London – Los Angeles –
Madrid – Miami – Shanghai – Tokyo – Washington, D.C.
Notable Projects: U.S. Capitol Visitor Center, Washington,
D.C.; LA Live!, Los Angeles, CA; Chinese Museum of Film,
Beijing, China; Texas Heart Institute, Houston, TX; John
Radcliffe Hospital, Oxford, UK.

SHW Group, LLP
Gary Keep, AIA; Mark Gerner, Associate AIA
5717 Legacy Drive
Plano, TX 75024
888.749.1019
www.shwgroup.com
Austin – Dallas – Detroit – Houston – San Antonio –
Washington, D.C.
Notable Projects: Emmett Conrad High School; Dallas
ISD; Northwest Stadium; Northwest ISD; Frisco Career and
Technology Education Center; Region X Education Service
Center; Little Elm High School.

TGS Architects
Dallas J. Taylor, AIA
5323 Spring Valley Road, Suite 200
Dallas, TX 75254
972.788.1945
www.tgsarchitects.com
Notable Projects: Jingu Mae retail tower, Tokyo; Mercer
Crossing Town Center, Dallas; Oak Cliff Bible Education
Center, Dallas; EDS Credit Union, Plano; Honolulu
Resort & Hotel.

Three
Gary P. Koerner, AIA; Frank A. Butler; Rockland Berg, AIA;
Carl S. Ede; Hunt Fugate, AIA; Brian J. McGauley
4040 North Central Expressway, Suite 200
Dallas, TX 75204
214.559.4080
www.threearch.com
Notable Projects: The Peninsula Beverly Hills, CA; Kahala
Nui Senior Living, Honolulu, HI; Fairmont Mayakoba Resort,
Riviera Maya; Fairmont Willow Stream Spa, Scottsdale, AZ;
The Umstead Hotel, Cary, NC.

Urban Design Group, Inc.
Ronald D. Armstrong, AIA; Raymond R. Kahl, AIA; John M.
Novack Jr., FAIA; Donald C. Buenger, AIA, LEED AP
15950 Dallas Parkway, Suite 325
Dallas, TX 75248
972.788.9242
www.urbandesigngroup.com
Atlanta – Dallas
Notable Projects: Wilderness Lodge, Orlando, FL;
Philbrook Museum of Art, Tulsa, OK; Carlson Center,
Minnetonka, MN; Rivercenter, San Antonio, TX; Tulsa
Community College: West Campus, Tulsa, OK.

WDG Architecture, Inc.
Sterling L. Little, AIA, Jamie Fernandez-Duran, AIA;
Vincent M. Hunter, AIA
325 North St. Paul, Suite 3800
Dallas, TX 75201
214.969.5311
www.wdgarch.com
Dallas – Washington, D.C.
Notable Projects: The Shore, Austin; Arlington Gateway,
Arlington, VA; The Milago, Austin; Centura Tower, Dallas;
Crystal City, Washington, D.C.; International Monetary
Fund Headquarters, Washington, D.C.

William Peck & Associates, Inc.
William Peck, AIA; Maria Isohanni, Associate AIA;
Yelena Ptashinskaya, Associate AIA; Lora Beth Robicheaux,
Associate AIA
105 West Main Street
Lewisville, TX 75057
972.221.1424
www.peckarchitects.com
Notable Projects: Bannister High Performance House;
Sunquist Office Building; Lynn Square Professional
Buildings, Ferguson House/Office; Heritage
Square Townhomes.

INDEX